CANTEEN
CUISINE

MARCO
PIERRE
WHITE

CANTEEN CUISINE
MARCO PIERRE WHITE
IN THE KITCHEN WITH MICHAEL CAINE

EBURY PRESS
LONDON

For my wife's friend Signor Chiandetti,
whose understanding helped turn my dreams into reality

First published in 1995

1 3 5 7 9 10 8 6 4 2

First published in the United Kingdom in 1995 by Ebury Press, Random House, 20 Vauxhall Bridge Road,
London SW1V 2SA

Random House Australia (Pty) Limited, 20 Alfred Street, Milsons Point, Sydney, New South Wales 2061,
Australia

Random House New Zealand Limited, 18 Poland Road, Glenfield, Auckland 10, New Zealand

Random House South Africa (Pty) Limited, PO Box 337, Bergvlei, South Africa

Random House UK Limited Reg. No. 95400

A CIP catalogue record for this book is available from the British Library

ISBN 0 09 180818 9

Edited by Susan Fleming
Designed by David Fordham
Photographs by Normand Hollands
Illustrations by Robert Edward
Index by Hilary Bird

Typeset by SX Composing Ltd, Rayleigh, Essex
Printed in Spain by Printer Industria Grafica SA, Barcelona

Papers used by Ebury Press are natural recyclable products made from wood grown in sustainable forests.

Contents

FOREWORD

THE RECIPES IN THIS BOOK all derive from The Canteen, a restaurant in London's Chelsea Harbour which I opened in partnership with Michael Caine in 1992. Running a successful restaurant needs two quite different skills. Obviously you have to understand food and be able to cook. But you also have to run the 'front of the house', manage the business side, and create an atmosphere in which people can relax and enjoy themselves and an ambience which will encourage them to return and to recommend the place to their friends. Of course the food matters enormously. But if the tables are too close together, or the acoustics are unsympathetic, or the decor is ugly, or the service is unfriendly, the delicious food will count for nothing. In learning about these skills I owe a huge debt to Michael.

He is of course one of the world's most famous film stars. He is also very interested in food, and extremely experienced in the running of restaurants, having over many years been an owner or part-owner of some first-rate and highly successful establishments. I am fortunate to count him as a friend.

When he and I met, I was running my first restaurant, Harvey's, in south-west London. This had certainly been successful for me, it had become quite well known for the quality of the food on offer there, and I had achieved some recognition as a chef both within the profession and outside. But I was still very young, both in years and in temperament. Meeting Michael changed my life. He showed extraordinary faith in me. He encouraged me to look beyond Wandsworth and to plan a new restaurant designed to bring top-class cooking to a level that a wider range of customers could afford. He was willing to invest in me, not only a substantial amount of money but his time, care, advice and commitment. The lessons I have learned from him are of inestimable value.

He introduced me to his friends and contacts in a world that to me at that time was unattainable, and thus enabled me to make further progress in my career. For example, through meeting Sir Rocco Forte I was able to move on from Harvey's to my new establishment, The Restaurant, in Forte's famous Hyde Park Hotel, where in due course I was to earn my third Michelin star. I suspect that if I had not met Michael Caine I could well still be cooking in Wandsworth.

His insights into the front-of-house skills in restaurant management derive in many ways from his consummate professionalism as an actor. For example, he taught me that in a restaurant the eye should always be stimulated by activity, whether from a waiter polishing a glass for the umpteenth time, or the slow movement of those 'colonial' fans suspended from the ceiling, or from television screens, or with the careful placing of mirrors on the walls. He taught me that when you walk into a restaurant you are walking onto a stage, with the eyes of the seated guests upon you, and when you take your seat at the table you join the audience. He taught me the virtues of calm and self-confidence: for example, he gave me a copy of his wonderful autobiography *What's It All About*, in which he had written 'If you don't let them see you sweat, you will win.' He taught me that in a restaurant no single person can create success, that everyone involved – whether it's the florist, the wine waiter, the maître-d, the waiter, the receptionist or the cook – plays a crucial part. As he puts it, 'success has many fathers, failure only one'.

Apart from the benefit I have had from his wisdom and experience, I have always derived huge pleasure from his company and his wit. Long ago he made a joke which still makes me laugh when I remember it. When we first opened The Canteen one of the waitresses, though fine-looking, was unusually tall. 'Marco,' said Michael. 'We'll have to stop her serving the food. She makes the portions look small!'

MARCO PIERRE WHITE
1995

INTRODUCTION

EVERYONE HAS TO COOK FOOD at some time in their lives, and millions of people do it every day. But not many people enjoy it much, and fewer still are any good at it. On the other hand, pretty well everybody knows how to appreciate and enjoy delicious food. So why don't more people enjoy cooking?

The main reason is that there's a gap between what they can do and what they enjoy eating. This is the gap between what we eat at home and what we eat on an evening out in a good restaurant. My aim in this book is to try and close this gap, to teach people how to enjoy what they do in the kitchen: to take that bit of extra care, to avoid those old pitfalls, to perfect their skills, and to produce a meal with that sense of joy and fulfilment we all get from doing something really well.

In a sense I have tried to do this, to bridge this gap, in the two restaurants I run in London. One of them is very expensive, and serves food which aims to reach the very highest possible standards of *haute cuisine*. It is based on classical French methods, we use only the finest and most expensive ingredients, and it caters for people who have a good deal of disposable income. My other restaurant is The Canteen in Chelsea Harbour, which I run with my partner Michael Caine. The main idea behind The Canteen is to bring down to an affordable level the cooking that we do at The Restaurant. And thus The Canteen epitomises what I hope to do in this book – to give the reader that confidence, that basic knowledge, to enable him or her to learn to enjoy the time they spend in the kitchen, not to mention eating the results afterwards.

Good cooking is a combination of several things – ingredients, skill, art, craft, imagination, and even a bit of science. Ingredients are certainly one of the most important factors, and at the top level we do use some very extravagant methods and materials. For instance, we use only large fish because they have more flavour. For rabbit we import specially reared animals from a particular district in France. Our meat and vegetables and herbs come from growers whose methods simply cost more than those of ordinary suppliers, because they are organic or because their standards are so high. We are profligate with things like truffles and caviare. When we make a wine sauce, we use fine wine rather than plonk.

But these refinements, although they can mean high prices, have less effect than you may think. It is perfectly possible to make magnificent food from ingredients bought in your local supermarket. The recipes I give in this book can virtually all, with very few exceptions, be made from raw materials that can be found in any high street. (Ten or fifteen years ago, when I started my career, this was certainly not the case – a sign of how far gastronomy – and people's palates – have progressed in Britain in a very short time.)

On the other hand it does pay to look around, to find those greengrocers who really care about the freshness of the produce they sell, those butchers who specialise in organic meat, those fishmongers whose prawns are fresh and not frozen, and who can still fillet a haddock with the old skill. It pays to use unsalted butter (which inexplicably costs more than salted), or fresh rather than dried mushrooms (though the latter have their place). Shopping in this way is also much more fun than pushing a trolley around a supermarket.

The skills, or the art or craft, of cooking can be acquired, and not necessarily through the conventional avenues – the catering colleges, apprenticeships, etc, the classical training. There are many highly skilled domestic cooks out there who have never had a formal day's tuition, but who can prepare and cook food, or write about it, with as much knowledge and finesse as a top-flight chef. I myself am largely self-taught, and indeed laid the foundation of my knowledge at the Box Tree in Ilkley, where Michael Lawson and Malcolm Read had no classical training whatsoever. What they did do was *eat*, taste, refine, remember and recreate. They had no technical knowledge, and all they could go on was instinct. They used to go to all the two- and three-star restaurants in France, and then would create their own way of achieving the flavours they had tasted. Michael Lawson was a great cook, and was the first Englishman ever to win two stars in the *Michelin Guide*. Funnily enough, he was born in Leeds, as was I – two Michelin-starred chefs from Leeds!

Although Michael Lawson perhaps came to dishes by unconventional means, it all worked, and I remember Albert Roux once saying that the best meal he'd ever eaten in

Britain was at the Box Tree. They would discover one route to a flavour or to a dish, and would perfect it, etch it in stone. This consistency was a major part of their success, but it was founded on skills that were more domestic in essence than professional. It just proves that, even if you haven't got the training, you can still follow your instincts to success.

Cookery books – collections of recipes from a particular chef or cook, or from a particular country or restaurant – can almost be classified as introductions to technique anyway. They may not define these in as much detail as the college manuals used by learner chefs, but they can be grasped by reading the recipes, as well as by attempting them. I believe, for instance, that by taking in the basic principles of the sauce recipes at the back of this book, you could create your own restaurant-style sauce in no time at all, using whatever ingredients you had to hand.

And by seeing and appreciating in those recipes what one culinary imagination has achieved, you can develop your own creative feeling for food, for its textures, flavours and combinations, for its basic simplicity. For instance, you could cook a turbot with grain mustard just as we do at The Canteen, in a matter of moments. Get a large Le Creuset dish, put in a knob of butter, chop your shallots, and cook without colouring. Deglaze with a little white wine and reduce for a minute or two; add fish stock, then put the turbot in, cover with a butter paper, and pop into the oven for 5 minutes. You've cooked it already. Pour off some of the juices, leave the fish to rest, and mount the juices with a little butter, a bit of cream to stabilise it, and a spoonful of grain mustard. It's as simple as that!

And a little scientific knowledge never goes astray either, especially in the kitchen. It's important to understand the general principles, and to be able to put them into practice, even if you don't necessarily know why. You know that you should seal a piece of meat or fish in fat in a pan before poaching or braising it. This closes the pores of the flesh so that the juices do not come out so much; and browning in fat, or caramelisation, will also add considerable flavour. To be a great cook, you don't need to know the exact chemistry or physics of *why* egg whites expand and stiffen when beaten; but you need to appreciate that that volume, if it is to be retained, needs to be handled carefully, whether to use in meringue or a soufflé. Although none of us at The Canteen are scientists, we do know a bit, and I hope the chef's notes throughout this book will help.

From science to equipment. Although most of these recipes can perfectly well be achieved in the domestic kitchen, I believe that home cooks are hampered in many ways.

11

For instance, I don't think they design a decent domestic stove – our professional ones are so much more efficient. Having said that, one of my earliest headaches at Harvey's (my first restaurant) concerned the aforementioned stove. When we first opened, in the winter, we'd be cooking away and at six in the evening the gas pressure would suddenly go low. We were in a highly residential area, and that was the time everyone would come home and turn on the gas, or their thermostats turned the central heating on. It was terrible – I couldn't even boil water!

As good a stove as you can afford is all I can advise, and always have it very well preheated. It may seem extravagant to turn it on half an hour in advance, but that consistency or intensity of heat will cook the soufflé or piece of fish to perfection. Another necessity in any kitchen is a good large roasting tray, preferably of aluminium, which bends back into shape after it cools (unlike stainless steel). One day it can cook roast chicken, the next it can poach some pieces of salmon or act as a bain-marie. Another vital thing is a good sieve, preferably a chinois, a coolie-hat-shaped sieve which lets all the liquid drain through the sides while the solids are trapped in the tip of the cone. Some chinois sieves have such a fine mesh that they can duplicate the function of muslin or cheesecloth.

What you need in order to be able to cook well – apart from good ingredients, good instincts, imagination, a little knowledge and good equipment – is a *love* of what you are doing and a love of eating. Those are the things that animate me more than anything else, as they do Michael Caine, my partner in The Canteen. Tim Payne, who cooks here, is as passionate about food as he is about Blackburn Rovers, and he, along with Peter Raffael and his team, has contributed enormously to this book. We all hope that the recipes we have selected will help you to enjoy cooking at home as much as we enjoy cooking for you at The Canteen.

STARTERS

STARTERS

THE STARTERS we serve at The Canteen exemplify many of the principles I am trying to get across in this book. None of the recipes is too difficult or too time-consuming (except perhaps for the terrines, but they have other advantages). Most of the ingredients are fairly easy to get hold of, although I must admit that a few are a little expensive. The recipes are varied: some are classics, dating from my very first days at Harvey's, some are influenced by other cuisines, and there is an admixture of hot and cold. Perhaps you'll feel that there are too many fish dishes; but then fish, with its multitude of flavours and textures, is always a favourite with cooks – well, with chefs anyway. We serve it as a starter in several ways, our tuna Niçoise is especially popular with Shakira Caine, the wife of my partner, Michael.

Shellfish are good too in the starter canon. Crab is a favourite of mine, and I like nothing better than choosing a big cock crab with big claws – the larger it is, the better the flavour – and cooking it in a court-bouillon for the requisite number of minutes, then taking it out of the liquid, draining, cooling and shelling. If you then make a mayonnaise (see page 204), and buy some brown bread from a good baker down the road, you've got one of the best possible meals. Crab meat is also useful in a number of other ways.

Oysters and champagne may not immediately appeal in a domestic culinary context, but the dish is simple to achieve and splendid in flavour. The roast sea scallops and calamari with a black squid ink sauce is a new concept, but it is simplicity itself to cook and serve. If you buy the best – and this is one reason for the Michelin star at The Canteen, our respect for good produce – then the cooking is and should be simple, to bring out those outstanding qualities. Eggs, poached or scrambled, come well within the remit of the domestic cook, and once those techniques have been perfected, as we show how to do in the recipes here, then you can play around with more exotic additions.

The soups too are very simple, but intense in flavour, and most have the addition of something tantalising, from all parts of the culinary spectrum – a poached egg, perhaps, or a langoustine tail, or ravioli of goat's cheese.

The terrines may seem difficult at first, and certainly may cost quite a lot to bring together, but they should work in a domestic sense as well as they do in a professional one, albeit slightly differently. You can – indeed *must* – make the terrine at least the day before, and this will leave you free to concentrate on other dishes on the day of your actual party.

VELOUTÉ OF CELERY
WITH POACHED EGG

4 PORTIONS

250 g (9 oz) celery, finely sliced
250 g (9 oz) celeriac, peeled
1 onion, peeled and finely sliced
1 white of leek, finely sliced
50 g (2 oz) unsalted butter
salt and freshly ground white pepper
100 g (4 oz) potatoes, peeled and finely sliced
500 ml (17 fl oz) double cream
500 ml (17 fl oz) Chicken Stock (SEE PAGE 190)

TO SERVE

4 eggs
finely chopped chives

1. Sweat the celery, celeriac, onion and leek in the butter without colouring, until all the moisture has evaporated. Season with salt and pepper.
2. Put the raw potato slices in a pan with the cream and stock, bring to the boil, and pour this over the rest of the vegetables. Cook on a high heat for about 10 minutes.
3. Liquidise the mixture, and pass it through a sieve. Check the seasoning.
4. To serve, poach the eggs (SEE PAGE 30), and place one in each soup plate. Pour the hot soup over, and sprinkle chopped chives on top.

CHEF'S NOTE

This is a great dish for the winter — it's comforting — and I can't think of anything better to come home to after a day's fishing or shooting. The celery has a good strong flavour, and the poached egg adds another dimension and texture.

4 PORTIONS

500 g (18 oz) white button mushrooms, finely sliced
1 small onion, peeled and finely sliced
1 white of leek, finely sliced
50 g (2 oz) unsalted butter
1 litre (1¾ pints) Chicken Stock (SEE PAGE 190)
500 ml (17 fl oz) double cream
100 g (4 oz) potatoes, peeled and finely sliced
salt and freshly ground white pepper

CAPPUCCINO OF MUSHROOMS

TO SERVE

12 crayfish tails
a few sprigs of chervil

1. Sweat the onion and leek in the butter over a low heat, without colouring them, and then add the mushrooms. Continue cooking until all the moisture has evaporated, still without colouring.
2. Put the chicken stock, cream and raw potato slices into a pan and bring to the boil. Pour this over the vegetables and cook on a medium heat for 10 minutes.
3. Liquidise the soup, and strain it through a sieve. If it's slightly too thick, add a little more chicken stock. Then season it with salt and pepper.
4. Steam the crayfish tails for 1 minute, and remove their shells. If not serving straight-away, set them aside in a warm place.
5. To serve, heat the soup until it is just short of boiling, then froth it with a hand blender for 2 minutes, to produce the 'cappuccino' effect. Pour into bowls over the crayfish tails, and sprinkle a little chervil over each.

MUSSEL SOUP

2 kg (4½ lb) mussels
1 onion, peeled and finely chopped
1 celery stalk, finely chopped
1 white of leek, finely chopped
25 g (1 oz) unsalted butter
1 teaspoon curry powder
½ teaspoon cayenne
1 sprig thyme
1 bay leaf
600 ml (1 pint) white wine
300 ml (10 fl oz) Fish Stock (SEE PAGE 192)
450 ml (15 fl oz) double cream
salt
1 pinch saffron strands

1. Wash the mussels, pull off their beards, and wash them again carefully.
2. Sweat the vegetables gently in the butter for 5 minutes. Add the curry powder, cayenne and herbs, and then the mussels, and continue cooking gently, with the lid on, for another minute.
3. Add the wine and stock, and cook for another few minutes until the mussels open. Pick the mussels out, and strain the stock through muslin or a very fine sieve.
4. In a clean pan, reduce the stock by half, then add the cream and reduce it further, to a coating consistency. Season with a little salt if required.
5. To serve, remove the mussels from their shells (making sure there are no beards), and place a few in each soup bowl. Heat the soup to just below boiling point, add the strands of saffron, and pour over the mussels.

Vegetables of the Seasons

8 PORTIONS

900 g (2 lb) salt cod
100 ml (3½ fl oz) olive oil
225 g (8 oz) potatoes, peeled and sliced
225 g (8 oz) white of leeks, thinly sliced
finely grated zest of ½ orange
1 sprig thyme
1.2 litres (2 pints) Fish Stock (SEE PAGE 192)
900 ml (1½ pints) water
600 ml (1 pint) double cream

SOUP OF BRANDADE

1. Dice the salt cod and leave in cold running water for 24 hours. This gets rid of most of the salt.

2. Drain the salt cod off and sauté gently in hot olive oil until all the water evaporates.

3. Add the potatoes and sauté until soft, about 5 minutes. Do not colour.

4. Add the leek, orange zest and thyme, and sweat for 4 minutes.

5. Pour in the fish stock and water, and bring to the boil. Skim and cook for another 10 minutes.

6. Blend, then push three times through a sieve. You must be sure to get rid of all the tiny bones.

7. To serve, add the cream, bring back to the boil, then pass again through a sieve.

750 g (1¾ lb) leeks (mainly white),
finely sliced
350 g (12 oz) onions, peeled and finely sliced
100 g (4 oz) unsalted butter
350 g (12 oz) potatoes, peeled and finely sliced
900 ml (1½ pints) Chicken Stock, boiling (SEE PAGE 190)
900 ml (1½ pints) water, boiling
200 ml (7 fl oz) double cream
salt and freshly ground white pepper
175 g (6 oz) smoked haddock
300 ml (10 fl oz) milk and water, mixed
chopped chives

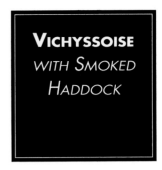

VICHYSSOISE WITH SMOKED HADDOCK

1. Sweat the leek and onion in the butter until they are soft, but without colouring them. Then add the finely sliced raw potato, the boiling stock and water, and cook over a fast heat for 10 minutes.

2. Add the cream and cook for a further 2 minutes. Liquidise then pass through a fine sieve. Season to taste.

3. Poach the haddock in the milk and water, a few minutes only, then drain and flake into large pieces.

4. To serve, put the sieved soup and chives into bowls, and divide the smoked haddock flakes between them. Serve immediately.

CHEF'S NOTE
This, in essence, is a simple idea — a leek and potato soup — but adding the smoked haddock takes it that little bit further down the road, it's an element of glamour.

GAZPACHO OF CRAB

4 PORTIONS

450 g (1 lb) plum tomatoes, seeded
½ cucumber, seeded
3 red peppers, seeded
1 onion, peeled
1½ garlic cloves, peeled
salt and freshly ground white pepper
50 ml (2 fl oz) sherry vinegar
a few drops of Tabasco
100 g (4 oz) fresh white crab meat

MAYONNAISE

500 ml (17 fl oz) olive oil
3 egg yolks

1. Make the mayonnaise in the usual way (SEE PAGE 204). It is to be used as a thickener, and you will not need it all (store in the fridge).
2. Chop the tomatoes, cucumber and peppers roughly, and put a little of each aside to use as the garnish. Dice this garnish.
3. Put the chopped vegetables, plus the chopped onion and garlic, into the food processor and blend. Push through a fine chinois sieve.
4. Season with a little salt and pepper, then add as much mayonnaise as is needed to thicken the soup. Adjust the seasoning, then add sherry vinegar and Tabasco to taste.
5. To serve, divide between soup plates, and garnish with the crab meat and the diced cucumber, red pepper and tomato.

450 g (1 lb) white crab meat
225 g (8 oz) brown crab meat
about 175 g (6 oz) Mayonnaise [SEE PAGE 204]
5 medium ripe avocados
lemon juice
4 plum tomatoes
a dash of Worcestershire sauce
a dash of Tabasco
salt and freshly ground white pepper

TO SERVE

1 recipe Sauce Gazpacho [SEE PAGE 205]
4 sprigs chervil

TIAN OF CRAB AND AVOCADO, *SAUCE GAZPACHO*

1. Keeping the crab meats separate, add just enough mayonnaise to each to bind together - about 50-75 g (2-3 oz) to the white meat, about 50 g (2 oz) to the brown.

2. Peel the avocados, remove the stones, and cut the flesh into 5 mm (¼ in) dice. Immediately cover with some lemon juice to prevent discoloration.

3. Blanch the tomatoes, then skin, seed and cut into 5 mm (¼ in) dice. In a large, round-bottomed bowl, mix together gently with the avocado, Worcestershire sauce, Tabasco and salt and pepper to taste.

4. To construct the tian, place a straight-sided pastry cutter, 10 cm (4 in) in diameter and 5 cm (2 in) deep, in the centre of the plate. Fill one-third of it with the avocado mix. On top place a thick layer of brown crab mayonnaise. On top of this place a thick layer of white crab mayonnaise. To finish, cover with a thin layer of plain mayonnaise, and level smooth.

5. To serve, surround the tian with the sauce and place a piece of chervil on top of the tian. Carefully remove the pastry cutter and serve.

CHEF'S NOTE

This recipe plays on the basic theme of crab mayonnaise. It's best served with slices of brioche toast — in fact I like it spread on toast.

RISOTTO OF INK
WITH ROAST CALAMARI

6 PORTIONS

300 g (11 oz) risotto rice (Carnaroli or Vialone)
50 g (2 oz) unsalted butter
1 shallot, peeled and chopped
4 x 25 ml (1 fl oz) packets squid ink
1 litre (1¾ pints) Fish Stock, boiling (SEE PAGE 192)
200 ml (7 fl oz) double cream, whipped
1 tablespoon freshly grated Parmesan
salt and freshly ground white pepper
lemon juice
fresh chervil

ROAST CALAMARI

100 g (4 oz) squid, cleaned and cut into julienne strips
100 ml (3½ fl oz) olive oil
a splash of white wine
25 g (1 oz) chopped parsley

1. Melt half the butter in a heavy-bottomed pan and sweat the shallot and rice in it for about 3-4 minutes.
2. Add the ink and half the fish stock, and cook the rice, adding more stock if required. Keep the rice moving as much as possible at all times to stop it sticking. When the rice is ready, almost all the liquid should have evaporated, and the grains should be *al dente*.
3. Bring the rice off the heat and add the remaining butter in pieces, the cream and the Parmesan. Season with salt, pepper and lemon juice to taste.
4. Meanwhile, fry the squid quickly in the olive oil to seal, but not to colour. Season, and add a little white wine and a little lemon juice, plus the parsley.
5. To serve, place the risotto in a bowl, making sure it falls flat - loosely rather than solidly - and place the squid on top. Garnish with the chervil.

CHEF'S NOTE

*T*his is an old favourite — one of those on which Harvey's built its reputation — which has found a new home at The Canteen.

4 PORTIONS

RISOTTO OF SEA SCALLOPS

8 medium sea scallops
300 g (11 oz) risotto rice (Carnaroli or Vialone)
1 shallot, peeled and finely chopped
olive oil
600 ml (1 pint) Scallop Stock, boiling (SEE PAGE 193)
120 g (4½ oz) Acid Butter (SEE PAGE 213)
1 tablespoon freshly grated Parmesan
1 carrot, peeled and cut into 5 mm (¼ in) dice
2 courgettes, green skin only, cut into 5 mm (¼ in) dice
salt and freshly ground white pepper
lemon juice
50 ml (2 fl oz) double cream, lightly whipped
15 g (½ oz) snipped chives
chervil sprigs

1. Cut the scallops into slices, and keep three good ones per portion. Cut the remainder into 5 mm (¼ in) dice.

2. Sweat the shallot in a tiny amount of olive oil in a heavy-bottomed pan for a few minutes, then add the rice. Stir for a few more minutes.

3. Add three-quarters of the boiling stock, and cook the rice, adding more stock if required. Keep the rice moving as much as possible at all times to stop it sticking. When the rice is ready, almost all the liquid should have evaporated and the grains should be *al dente*.

4. Meanwhile fry the scallop slices briefly in a little olive oil to sear and brown, a few moments only.

5. Whisk the acid butter and the Parmesan into the risotto. Stir in the vegetable dice and the scallop dice, and season to taste with salt, pepper and lemon juice.

6. Add the cream and chives at the very last moment, and remove immediately from the heat.

7. To serve, place the risotto in a bowl as in the last recipe, and garnish with the scallop slices and the chervil.

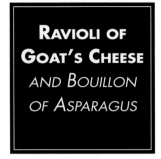

RAVIOLI OF GOAT'S CHEESE *AND BOUILLON OF ASPARAGUS*

4 PORTIONS

450 g (1 lb) fresh asparagus
¼ onion, peeled and chopped
½ celery stalk, chopped
1 sprig thyme
1 bay leaf
50 g (2 oz) unsalted butter
salt and freshly ground white pepper
500 ml (17 fl oz) Chicken Stock (SEE PAGE 190)
500 ml (17 fl oz) Vegetable Stock (SEE PAGE 193)

RAVIOLI OF GOAT'S CHEESE

½ recipe Fresh Pasta (SEE PAGE 215)
250 g (9 oz) firm goat's cheese
1 tablespoon Mascarpone cheese
100 g (4 oz) Chicken Mousse (SEE PAGE 214)
1 egg yolk
olive oil

1. Make the ravioli filling by combining the cheeses and binding them with the chicken mousse.

2. To make the ravioli, roll out the fresh pasta until paper thin, and cut into four large circles. Place the filling on one half, and fold the other half over, sticking the edges firmly together with a smear of egg yolk, to make a half-moon shape. Trim if necessary. (The ravioli can, in fact, be any shape you like.)

3. To start the bouillon, remove the asparagus tips. Blanch them in boiling water. Refresh in cold water, drain, and set aside until later.

4. Lightly chop the peeled asparagus stalks with the onion and celery in a blender, then put into a pan with the thyme, bay leaf and butter. Season, and cook gently until soft. Then add the stocks, bring to the boil and simmer for 10 minutes. Pass through a chinois sieve, and reserve the bouillon, discarding the vegetables.

5. To cook the ravioli, add a little olive oil to a pan of boiling salted water, and place them gently in it for 2 minutes. Then refresh them in cold water, and place on a tray. When ready to serve, cook them for 5 more minutes in boiling water.

6. To serve, heat the bouillon and skim off any fat from the surface. Put a raviolo in each bowl with some asparagus tips, and pour the hot bouillon over.

4 PORTIONS

24 x No. 2 langoustines
½ recipe Fresh Pasta (SEE PAGE 215)
salt and freshly ground white pepper
about 30 basil leaves
1 egg, beaten
olive oil

TO SERVE

½ recipe Sweet and Sour Pineapple Cream
(SEE PAGE 201)
2 courgettes, diced
6 plum tomatoes, skinned, seeded and diced
2 apples, peeled, cored and diced
25 g (1 oz) unsalted butter

(SEE PAGE 215)
(SEE PAGE 201)

RAVIOLI OF LANGOUSTINE WITH SWEET AND SOUR PINEAPPLE CREAM

1. To prepare the langoustines, remove the heads, gently press the tails and peel off the shells. Remove the waste pipes and trim any loose flesh.

2. To prepare the ravioli, roll the fresh pasta out so that it becomes almost transparent. Divide into 24 roughly similarly sized pieces.

3. Place two pieces of langoustine on one piece of pasta, season and place a basil leaf on top. Brush around with egg wash, and place another layer of pasta on top. Press around the edges and cut out using a suitable 7.5 cm (3 in) cutter. Chill until required.

4. Warm the sauce through gently.

5. Cook the ravioli in salted boiling water with a touch of olive oil for about 4 minutes.

6. Quickly toss the vegetables in the butter, then season lightly. Place in the bottom of a dish, place three cooked ravioli per person on top, and cover with sauce. Decorate with the remaining basil leaves.

CHEF'S NOTE

Years ago at Harvey's, one of the specialities was roast langoustines with cracked white peppercorns and a sauce of caramelised pineapple. This was the inspiration for this Canteen adaptation.

Oeufs Meurette

4 PORTIONS

8 very fresh, free-range eggs
red wine vinegar

TO SERVE

4 round slices Brioche (SEE PAGE 217)
100 g (4 oz) unsalted butter
50 g (2 oz) each of fresh morels, fresh girolles and
button mushrooms
salt and freshly ground black pepper
2 medium tomatoes, skinned, seeded and diced
24 Roast Button Onions (SEE PAGE 207)
1 recipe Red Wine Sauce (SEE PAGE 195)
24 each of tarragon and chervil leaves and chive ends

1.   Have ready a deep poaching pan, not too wide, and fill two-thirds of it with water. Bring up to about 90°C/194°F, simmering, and add some red wine vinegar (approximately ⅛ of the volume of the water).

2.   Crack the eggs one at a time into a cup and turn into the simmering water. If the pan is large enough, you could do 4 eggs at a time. The white and the yolk will sink to the bottom and excess white and scum will come to the top. Skim this off. The eggs will be ready in about 2-2½ minutes, but *feel* to see if the yolk is soft and the white cooked.

3.   If not using straightaway, lift out with a slotted spoon and store in a cloth temporarily, or in a bowl of lightly acidulated and iced water (a few more drops of red wine vinegar). You can trim the edges of the white before reheating in hot water when required.

4.   Pan-fry the slices of brioche in half the butter until golden brown on both sides. Keep warm.

5.   Quarter the button mushrooms, then sauté all the mushrooms in the remaining butter. Season, and add the raw tomato dice at the last minute.

6.   Reheat the eggs, onions and sauce.

7.   To serve, place the brioche in the centre of the plate with the eggs, two per person, on top. Place the onions and mushrooms over and around. Spoon around the sauce, and garnish with the herbs.

4 PORTIONS

12 eggs
60 g (2¼ oz) unsalted butter
salt
50 ml (2 fl oz) double cream

TO SERVE

100 g (4 oz) sea urchins
4 sprigs chervil

SCRAMBLED EGGS
WITH SEA URCHIN

1. Beat the eggs lightly together with a fork.
2. Melt the butter over a medium heat in a heavy-bottomed non-stick pan, pour in the eggs and stir constantly with a wooden spoon. As they start to thicken, season with salt and continue cooking.
3. As soon as the eggs are thick but still loose, stir in the cream to lighten them and stop the cooking. Remove from the heat.
4. Meanwhile, preheat the grill. Cut the sea urchins open, using scissors, to reveal the yellow or orange tongues or strips of flesh.
5. Smear a non-stick tray with a little extra butter, and place the sea urchin tongues on it. Grill them lightly for 30 seconds or so, just enough to heat them up a little.
6. To serve, pour the scrambled eggs into bowls. Place the sea urchin tongues on top and garnish with a sprig of chervil.

CHEF'S NOTE
If you can't find sea urchins, you can garnish scrambled eggs with poached oysters, smoked salmon or girolles with a provençale sauce. They're also delicious with or on toast, of course.

SPRING ROLLS
WITH CRAB

6 PORTIONS

vegetable oil for deep-frying
300 g (11 oz) white crab meat
2 red peppers   1 bunch spring onions
sesame oil
75 g (3 oz) fresh root ginger
about 2 dessertspoons Mayonnaise (SEE PAGE 204)
soy sauce
salt and freshly ground white pepper
12 sheets filo pastry
100 ml (3½ fl oz) clarified butter

TO SERVE

24 coriander leaves

1. Heat a deep-fryer to 180°C/350°F.
2. Clean the crab meat, checking for pieces of shell.
3. Place the red peppers under a hot grill until the skin blisters, being careful not to burn the flesh. Peel and cut the flesh into tiny dice.
4. Top and tail the spring onions and cut half of them into fine julienne strips (leave in iced water to 'curl' up), and the other half finely on the bias. Sweat this latter in about 1 tablespoon sesame oil until soft, then drain.
5. Cut the ginger into fine julienne strips, then blanch in boiling water. Refresh in cold water, then dry on kitchen paper.
6. Combine the crab meat, ginger and cooked spring onions, then add just enough mayonnaise to bind. Season with a little soy sauce and some pepper.
7. Fold the filo sheets in half, one at a time, and brush the top with a little clarified butter. Keep the remaining filo sheets covered with a damp cloth. Still one at a time, place some of the mixture on the folded sheet, leaving 2.5 cm (1 in) at the bottom edge and sides. First fold the sides in, then the bottom edge, then roll tightly up. Repeat with the remaining filo sheets and the remaining crab mix.
8. Mix 2 tablespoons sesame oil and 1 tablespoon soy sauce together, then mix in the pepper dice. Use this to make a circle on the plates.
9. Dress the 'curled' julienne of spring onion with a little lemon juice and salt and pepper. Place half in the middle of the plates.
10. Drop the spring rolls into the deep-fryer and cook until golden brown, about 2 minutes. Drain well on absorbent kitchen paper, then season. The outside should be crisp with the middle warm.
11. To serve, put the spring rolls in the middle of the plates, with the remaining spring onion and the coriander on top.

4 PORTIONS

20 oysters
salt
200 ml (7 fl oz) champagne
1 recipe Velouté for Fish (SEE PAGE 198)

TO SERVE

25 g (1 oz caviar (optional)
20 tiny sprigs chevil

OYSTERS
WITH
CHAMPAGNE
SABAYON

1. Remove the oysters from their shells carefully, and pass the juice through a piece of muslin into a bowl. Quickly wash each oyster in lightly salted water to remove any remaining bits of shell, and place in the juice.

2. Boil the bottom shells, and clean them thoroughly.

3. Poach the oysters in the champagne and a little of their own juices for no longer than 45 seconds on each side. Do not allow them to boil (they are best if kept below 80°C/176°F).

4. Remove the oysters, turn up the heat and rapidly reduce the cooking liquor by half. Lower the heat, add the velouté sauce, and cook until it reaches a coating consistency. Froth it with a hand blender.

5. To serve, place one hot oyster in each shell and pour some sauce over the top. Put ½ teaspoon caviar on each oyster, plus a sprig of chervil.

ROAST SEA SCALLOPS AND CALAMARI, SAUCE NERO

4 PORTIONS

12 medium sea scallops, cleaned
24 baby squid, cleaned
salt and freshly ground white pepper
olive oil
lemon juice

TO SERVE

1 recipe Sauce Nero (SEE PAGE 200)

1. Slice each scallop in half and season with salt. Heat a little oil in a non-stick pan, and carefully place the scallops in to cook for 1 minute on each side. Squeeze one or two drops of lemon juice over each scallop, and remove from the heat.

2. Cook the baby squid in a little olive oil in another non-stick pan until crisp, a minute or so, then season with a little salt.

3. To serve, arrange the scallops around the plate, each with a baby squid on top, and dot the black sauce around them (most effective on a white plate!). This dish can be garnished with deep-fried vegetables or herbs.

Start the salmon at least 48 hours in advance

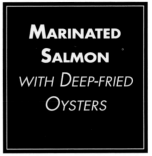

MARINATED SALMON *WITH DEEP-FRIED OYSTERS*

6 PORTIONS

12 oysters
100 g (4 oz) Chinese self-raising flour
salt and freshly ground white pepper
iced water
vegetable oil for deep-frying

MARINATED SALMON

450 g (1 lb) fresh salmon fillet in the piece, skin on
150 g (5 oz) salt   50 g (2 oz) caster sugar
5 g (⅛ oz) coriander seeds, lightly crushed
5 g (⅛ oz) white peppercorns, lightly crushed
1 bunch dill, chopped
juice and finely grated zest of 2 lemons
juice and finely grated zest of 1 orange
Dijon mustard
1 bunch lemon balm, chopped

TO SERVE

1 recipe Citrus Butter Sauce (SEE PAGE 201)
fresh chervil   sea salt

1. Make the marinade for the salmon by mixing the salt, sugar, coriander, peppercorns, half the dill, and the citrus juices and zests. Cover the salmon with this, cover with cling film, and leave to marinate for 24 hours.
2. Wash off the marinade, brush the salmon thinly with mustard, and cover it with lemon balm and the rest of the dill. Cover with cling film and press down with a heavy weight, to aid the absorption of the aromatics. Leave for another 24 hours.
3. For the oyster batter, place the flour in a bowl, with a pinch of salt, and whisk in enough iced water (about 150 ml/5 fl oz) to make a good batter consistency. Rest for 5 minutes in the fridge, then whisk again before use.
4. Dip the oysters in the batter and deep-fry them in very hot vegetable oil for about 1 minute until golden and crisp. Drain well, then season with salt.
5. To serve, slice the salmon as thinly as possible with a very sharp knife, and arrange slices down the centre of each plate. Put the drained and seasoned oysters in the centre top and bottom. Serve with the citrus butter sauce. Garnish with strands of fresh chervil and a sprinkling of sea salt.

BALLOTINE OF SALMON

ABOUT 14 PORTIONS

1 x 4.5-5.4 kg (10-12 lb) salmon, filleted and skinned
salt and freshly ground white pepper
cayenne pepper
2 bunches each of chervil, chives, tarragon, dill and flat parsley, finely chopped
1½ leaves bronze-leaf gelatine

TO SERVE

about 225 g (8 oz) Fromage Blanc with Herbs (SEE PAGE 214)
25 g (1 oz) Keta salmon eggs   chervil sprigs

1. Season the salmon fillets on both sides with salt, pepper and cayenne, and leave for 15 minutes. Dry with kitchen paper to remove the liquid.
2. Meanwhile, lay out two sheets of cling film, one-third overlapping, to measure about 5 cm (2 in) longer than the salmon. Lay out another two sheets of cling film in exactly the same manner on top of the first two.
3. Place half the chopped herbs on top of the cling film and press the skin side of one salmon fillet on to the herbs. Place the gelatine leaves on top of this piece of salmon.
4. Place the other half of the salmon 'head to tail' on top of the bottom piece, skin side up. Coat with the remaining herbs.
5. Roll tightly lengthwise in cling film to a sausage shape, then tie off both ends, being careful to exclude as much air as possible. Tie the salmon at three equal intervals to maintain its shape. Roll in a wet tea towel, and tie in the same way. Weigh the salmon.
6. To cook, poach in heavily seasoned water to cover for 3 minutes per 450 g (1 lb) at 65°C/149°F. Leave to cool for 1 hour in the liquor, then remove from the liquor. Cool completely, then refrigerate for 24 hours.
7. To serve, remove the cloth and cling film. Cut very carefully into the relevant number of slices. Place a slice just below the centre of each plate with a quenelle of fromage blanc and a little mound of Keta. Garnish with chervil.

CHEF'S NOTE

This also makes a nice main course in the summer, ideal for a dinner party, as it can be prepared 24 hours in advance. You can use a smaller salmon, but not below 3.6 kg (8 lb) on the bone, or larger than 6.3 kg (14 lb).

COMPOTE OF SALMON AND CAULIFLOWER CREAM

6 PORTIONS

1 side of salmon, about 1.1 kg (2½ lb), skinned, filleted and pin-boned
1 litre (1¾ pints) extra virgin olive oil
1 bunch dill   1 teaspoon rock salt

CAULIFLOWER CREAM

1 medium cauliflower
milk
a handful of fresh coriander
1 teaspoon coriander seeds, crushed
1 teaspoon white peppercorns, crushed
500 ml (17 fl oz) double cream
salt and freshly ground white pepper

TO SERVE

a handful of seasonal salad leaves
100 ml (3½ fl oz) Vinaigrette (SEE PAGE 206)
6 slices toasted Brioche (SEE PAGE 217)

1.   Preheat the oven to 90°C/194°F/the very lowest gas.
2.   Place the salmon in a suitable container lined with foil, and cover with the olive oil and fresh dill. Sprinkle with rock salt. Fold the foil over and place the container in a preheated oven, making sure that the salmon is completely immersed in the oil. The cooking time will be around 20 minutes. The salmon should then be taken out of the oven and left in the oil.
3.   To make the cauliflower cream, break the cauliflower into small florets, and place in a pan with enough milk to cover. Tie the fresh coriander and crushed seeds and peppercorns in a small piece of muslin and place in the milk. Cook until the cauliflower florets are very soft.
4.   Drain off and discard the milk, remove and discard the small muslin bag, then purée the cauliflower.
5.   Leave to cool, then gently fold in the double cream. Season as required, then chill.
6.   Gently remove the salmon from the oil, removing any dill. Drain off any excess oil, then gently flake the salmon.
7.   To serve, place a 10 cm (4 in) ring mould on the first plate. Place some flaked salmon in the bottom of the mould. Spoon the chilled cauliflower cream on top and garnish with a small seasonal salad and toasted brioche. Remove the mould and create compotes of salmon on the other plates.

4 PORTIONS

4 x 100 g (4 oz) pieces of fresh tuna
olive oil
salt and freshly ground white pepper

NIÇOISE SALAD

100 g (4 oz) small new potatoes
75 ml (2½ fl oz) Vinaigrette (SEE PAGE 206)
12 stoned black olives
8 anchovy fillets
100 g (4 oz) thin French beans, cooked
3 tomatoes, skinned, seeded and cut into strips
2 hard-boiled eggs
50 ml (2 fl oz) balsamic vinegar
4 sprigs chervil

TUNA NIÇOISE

1. Boil the new potatoes until cooked. Slice them, and marinate them while still warm in the vinaigrette for at least an hour.
2. Put the potatoes, olives, anchovies, beans and tomato into a bowl.
3. Pan-fry the tuna in a little of the olive oil until medium cooked, about 2 minutes on each side.
4. Peel and cut each hard-boiled egg into six wedges, and put three on each plate.
5. Mix 200 ml (7 fl oz) olive oil and the balsamic vinegar. Toss most of this into the bowl of vegetables, then arrange the vegetables on each plate on top of the eggs. Sprinkle with the chervil leaves.
6. Place the fish on top of the vegetables, and sprinkle with the rest of the oil and balsamic vinegar mixture.

CHEF'S NOTE

This is normally served as a starter but it would make a wonderful main course in the summer, with a slightly larger piece of tuna, and an expanded salad.

CARPACCIO OF TUNA,
SALAD OF HERBS

Start this dish at least 8 hours in advance.

6-8 PORTIONS

1 x 275 g (10 oz) loin of tuna, 4 cm (1½ in) in diameter
olive oil
25 ml (1 fl oz) soy sauce
25 g (1 oz) Dijon mustard
25 g (1 oz) each of chopped parsley, coriander, dill and
chives

SALAD OF HERBS

1 head oakleaf lettuce
1 head frisée endive
1 bunch wild rocket
100 ml (3½ fl oz) Vinaigrette (SEE PAGE 206)
20 each of chervil sprigs, tarragon leaves and chive ends

TO SERVE

fleur de sel
freshly ground white pepper
50 ml (2 fl oz) olive oil
50 ml (2 fl oz) balsamic vinegar
juice of 1 lime

1. Carefully trim all blood and sinew from the tuna. In a hot pan, using about 50 ml (2 fl oz) olive oil, quickly seal all round the outside of the tuna. Remove from the pan.
2. Mix the soy sauce and mustard together and brush the tuna all over to give a thin coating.
3. Mix all the chopped herbs together and roll the tuna in them. Roll the tuna very tightly in cling film into a long roulade shape. Allow this to rest for 8 hours to help form and set the shape.
4. Wash the hearts of the lettuces and pick out any tattered leaves or tough stalks. Do not bruise the lettuce. Dry well but carefully.
5. To serve, slice the tuna thinly with the cling film on, then remove the cling film and arrange a few slices on each plate. Toss the salad leaves lightly in the vinaigrette and place neatly in the centre of the plate.
6. Season the tuna with *fleur de sel* and pepper, lightly spoon olive oil and balsamic vinegar around, and sprinkle the tuna with a few drops of lime juice. Arrange the chervil, tarragon and chives neatly over the tuna and salad.

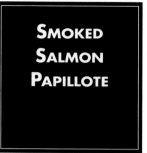

SMOKED SALMON PAPILLOTE

6 PORTIONS

*6 x 2-3 mm (⅛ in) thick slices of smoked salmon, approx
13 x 16 m (5¼ x 6½ in)*

MOUSSE

*300 g (11 oz) smoked salmon
625 ml (21 fl oz) thick double cream
cayenne pepper
juice of ½ lemon
salt if required*

TO SERVE

*olive oil
12 slices toasted Brioche (SEE PAGE 217)*

1. Place the smoked salmon slices individually between two sheets of baking parchment, and refrigerate until required.
2. To make the mousse, purée the smoked salmon in a food processor, then push through a fine drum sieve. Refrigerate thoroughly.
3. In a large, round-bottomed bowl over ice, fold the double cream into the sieved smoked salmon. Add a generous pinch of cayenne and the lemon juice. Taste for seasoning and add salt if necessary (depending on the saltiness of the smoked salmon). Refrigerate thoroughly.
4. To construct the papillote, remove the top sheet of baking parchment from one of the smoked salmon slices, leaving the bottom piece of parchment in place.
5. Place a 150 g (5 oz) quantity of mousse about 2 cm (1½ in) from the short side of the sliced salmon. Roll the parchment and salmon up to make a sausage shape. Leaving the 'log' on one end of the parchment, peel back the parchment and discard.
6. With the back of a knife gently push the ends of the log down and inwards to form a plump, pillow-shaped parcel. Cover in baking parchment and refrigerate until required.
7. To serve, place the papillote just below the centre of a plate, brush with olive oil and serve with two slices of toasted brioche.

15 GENEROUS PORTIONS

175 g (6 oz) York ham
175 g (6 oz) Bayonne ham
175 g (6 oz) smoked duck
500 g (18 oz) mixed wild mushrooms
100 ml (3½ fl oz) olive oil
3 large Savoy cabbages
salt and freshly ground white pepper
15 sage leaves, cut thinly
unsalted butter
1 sprig rosemary
1 sprig thyme
1 large garlic clove, peeled and finely chopped
3 shallots, peeled and finely chopped
600 g (1¼ lb) fresh foie gras

TO SERVE

Madeira Jelly (SEE PAGE 194)
25 ml (1 fl oz) truffle oil
250 ml (8 fl oz) olive oil

TERRINE D'HIVER

1. Cut the hams and smoked duck into small julienne strips, then set aside.
2. Pick over and wash the wild mushrooms as necessary. Dry well, then sauté in olive oil to soften. Set aside.
3. Remove and discard the outermost leaves of the cabbages. Strip off the remainder of the cabbage leaves, discarding only the very white leaves in the centre. Cut out the large stalks. Cut the leaves roughly, wash, and set aside.
4. Line a terrine, 30 x 11 cm (12 x 4½ in) and 10 cm (4 in) deep, with two layers of cling film, leaving a generous overlap.
5. To prepare the cabbage, blanch in boiling salted water, then refresh and drain.
6. Place the cabbage, sage and 100 g (4 oz) of the butter in a pan with a tight-fitting lid and steam for about 15 minutes. Remove to a large bowl and cover with cling film. Keep warm.
7. To prepare the mushrooms, blanch the rosemary leaves, then chop very finely with the thyme. Sauté the mushrooms with the rosemary, thyme, garlic and shallots in 50 g (2 oz) of the butter. Remove to a bowl, cover with cling film and keep warm.
8. To prepare the foie gras, cut it into slices approximately 1.5 cm (¾ in) thick, then sauté a little at a time in a hot pan to colour nicely. Remove the foie gras and keep warm.
9. Pass the foie gras juices and fat through a fine sieve into a large bowl containing 100 g (4 oz) butter which you have melted.

10. To start the assembly, into this bowl place enough cabbage to cover the bottom of the terrine, and heavily season it. Ladle the melted butter and foie gras fat over the cabbage. Make sure the leaves are well coated, then drain the fat back into the bowl. Press the leaves into the terrine with the back of the hand.

11. In the same bowl place the York ham. Ladle the melted butter and foie gras over it, and then drain back into the bowl. Place the ham strips into the terrine in the same way, on top of the cabbage. After these two layers, coat the other ingredients individually in the butter and foie gras fat, drain and then arrange in the terrine in the following order. Do not season the Bayonne or smoked duck layers.

cabbage	Bayonne	cabbage	smoked duck
foie gras	cabbage	foie gras	cabbage
cabbage	mushrooms	cabbage	

The finished result should come 1-1.5 cm (½-¾ in) over the top of the terrine mould.

12. Wrap the overlapping cling film over the top of the terrine and pierce many holes along the top edges of the film. Place a board on top of the terrine and press with about 4.5 kg (10 lb) of weight for 2 hours. Refrigerate for 24 hours.

13. Meanwhile, pour a little liquid Madeira jelly into each serving plate and allow to set.

14. To serve, turn the terrine out of the mould, using the cling film, then remove the film. Slice and place each slice on the plate on top of the set jelly, just below the centre. Brush with a mixture of the truffle and olive oils.

CHEF'S NOTE

This is an expensive, complicated and time-consuming dish, but well worth making for a special occasion. Make it at least the day before, and chill until needed. For the greatest success, as you are using melted butter and foie gras fat, you must work swiftly.

TERRINE OF SWEETBREADS AND CHICKEN,
SAUCE GRIBICHE

14-15 PORTIONS

enough Parma ham to line the mould, thinly sliced
700 g (1½ lb) chicken fillets, cut in strips
olive oil
500 g (18 oz) fresh foie gras, sliced
800 g (1¾ lb) calf's sweetbreads, trimmed
190 g (6¾ oz) baby onions, peeled
100 g (4 oz) trompettes
150 g (5 oz) girolles
salt and freshly ground white pepper
500 ml (17 fl oz) Chicken Stock (SEE PAGE 190)
4 gelatine leaves, soaked in cold water to soften
50 ml (2 fl oz) sherry vinegar

TO SERVE

3 recipes Sauce Gribiche (SEE PAGE 205)
40 tarragon leaves
chervil sprigs

1. Preheat the oven to 90°C/194°F/the very lowest gas.
2. Line a terrine mould, 30 x 8 cm (12 x 3½ in) and 8 cm (3½ in) deep, with three layers of cling film. Arrange the thinly sliced Parma ham on the inside, overlapping slightly, until the terrine is fully lined.
3. Seal the chicken fillets by sautéing in a little olive oil. Drain well. Sauté the sliced foie gras for a few minutes. Wrap the sweetbreads in cling film and cook until firm in boiling water. Refresh in iced water. Remove the film.
4. Blanch and refresh the baby onions. Prepare and wash the two types of mushroom, and dry off well.
5. When all the ingredients have been prepared, layer them into the terrine to achieve a mosaic effect (see the photograph), making sure that each layer is well seasoned. Pour in the chicken stock.
6. Place the terrine in a bain-marie, cover the top of the terrine with foil, and cook in the preheated oven for 1 hour, 25 minutes.
7. When cooked, strain off the stock from the terrine. Add the gelatine and sherry vinegar to the stock, and pour back into the terrine. Cool, then refrigerate to set.
8. To serve, turn the terrine out of the mould, and slice carefully. Pour a little sauce on to each plate, and place a slice of the terrine on top. Garnish with tarragon leaves and chervil sprigs.

CABBAGE À L'ANCIENNE, SAUCE TOMATE

4 PORTIONS

2 Savoy cabbages
salt and freshly ground white pepper
1 recipe Tomato Sauce (SEE PAGE 204)

STUFFING

150 g (5 oz) pork fat, chopped
150 g (5 oz) lean pork, chopped
25 g (1 oz) chicken livers, trimmed
½ clove garlic, peeled and crushed
½ tablespoon chopped parsley
10 g (¼ oz) breadcrumbs
25 ml (1 fl oz) white wine
½ tablespoon brandy
½ egg

BRAISING LIQUOR

1 carrot, peeled   1 onion, peeled
1 celery stalk   2 garlic cloves, peeled
1 bay leaf   1 sprig thyme
2 tablespoons olive oil
100 ml (3½ fl oz) white wine
500 ml (7 fl oz) Veal Stock (SEE PAGE 192)

1. Mince together the meats, then mix in the remaining ingredients of the stuffing.
2. Take twelve leaves from the outside of the cabbages, and remove the main vein. Then, using 10, 7.5 and 5 cm (4, 3 and 2 in) cutters, cut out four pieces of leaf in each of the three sizes.
3. Spread each circular leaf evenly with the stuffing mixture. Lie each 7.5 cm (3 in) piece on a 10 cm (4 in), and each 5 cm (2 in) on top. Place each lot of leaves (in turn) on a square of doubled cling film. Pull the corners shut and twist so that the cling film forms a ball with the cabbage inside doing the same. Make four balls in all.
4. Dice all the braising liquor vegetables and cook them gently in a medium pan in the oil until brown. Add the wine, turn up the heat and boil to reduce by about half. Add the stock and bring to the boil. Strain, discarding the vegetables.
5. Braise the cabbage balls in this liquor for about 1 hour, 20 minutes.
6. Meanwhile, make or heat through the tomato sauce.
7. To serve, place each cabbage ball in the centre of a bowl, and pour the tomato sauce carefully around it.

This luxurious pâté must be made 24 hours in advance.

15 GENEROUS PORTIONS

400 g (14 oz) fresh foie gras
400 g (14 oz) fresh chicken livers
200 ml (7 fl oz) ruby port
200 ml (7 fl oz) Madeira
100 ml (3½ fl oz) brandy
300 g (11 oz) shallots, peeled and finely sliced
3 garlic cloves, peeled and finely sliced
2 generous sprigs thyme
sel rose (pink sea salt)
white sea salt
8 eggs, at room temperature
800 g (1¾ lb) unsalted butter, melted and just above
blood heat

TO FINISH AND SERVE

150 g (5 oz) unsalted butter
Madeira Jelly (SEE PAGE 194)
coarsely ground white pepper

1. Preheat the oven to 160°C/325°F/Gas 3, and have ready a terrine or pâté mould 30 x 11 cm (12 x 4½ in), and 10 cm (4 in) deep.
2. Place the port, Madeira and brandy in a pan with the shallot, garlic and thyme, and boil to reduce until almost dry. Remove the thyme.
3. Slice the foie gras and chop the chicken livers. Place in a pan and warm to just above blood heat, covered with 1 level dessertspoon of sel rose and 1 level tablespoon of white sea salt.
4. Place the port mixture and the livers into a liquidiser and blend until fully liquidised. You may need to do this in batches.
5. Add the eggs, and mix well.
6. Add and mix in the warm melted butter then, working quickly, push through a chinois sieve into a warm container. Transfer to the terrine, and cover tightly with a piece of kitchen foil.
7. Place in a bain-marie, and cook in the preheated oven for 1 hour, 10 minutes.
8. Remove from the bain-marie, cool, and then refrigerate for 24 hours.
9. To finish, melt a quarter of the butter, and soften the remainder. Emulsify together by whisking; this lightens the butter.

CHICKEN LIVER AND FOIE GRAS PARFAIT

10. Spread a thin layer of this light butter on top of the parfait, then chill to set. Run a hot knife around the edges and turn out on to a board. (If it is difficult to get out, it may be sticking on the bottom. Put a tea towel over it, and pour on some boiling water. This will loosen it. Butter the other sides of the parfait in exactly the same way, then chill to set.

11. Meanwhile, pour a little liquid Madeira jelly into the chosen serving plates, and allow to set.

12. To serve, slice the parfait with a hot knife, and place a slice just below the centre of the plate, on top of the set jelly. Sprinkle with a little sea salt and coarsely ground white pepper. Offer slices of good, crusty, country bread as accompaniment.

CHEF'S NOTE

The sel rose helps retain the colour of the livers; the white salt is the seasoning. To gild the lily, you could include a chopped black truffle in the parfait mixture before cooking. This recipe may seem expensive, but in fact the only thing that costs anything worth mentioning is the foie gras itself.

58

FISH

FISH

I N RESTAURANTS, the general emphasis for main courses must be on dishes that can be prepared fairly quickly, to order, and this is reflected to a great extent in these Canteen recipes. Once again, we use prime quality ingredients, but the cooking techniques involved are not difficult, and indeed most are very easy. It is often the accompaniments for a perfect piece of fish – the sauces and vegetable garnishes, for instance – that take longer to prepare, but in most cases these can be readied in advance, requiring only gentle reheating, which means less work at the vital time of service.

As with the starters, there are many fish recipes, and I think you will find a huge variety of ideas here. There are several recipes involving salmon, for instance, but I firmly believe that salmon is the most versatile of fish: it smokes well, poaches well, pan-fries and grills very well; it can be served hot or cold; and it has a fabulous flavour. I haven't actually included one of the most effective ways of cooking it: on a hot summer's day, cold poached salmon, with mayonnaise and hot new potatoes, has to be the best. It's simply a matter of dropping the cleaned fish into a court-bouillon brought up to 100°C/212°F, and then taking it off the heat. The fish brings the temperature of the liquid down to 70°C/158°F, which is the temperature at which fish protein cooks. The secret then is to leave the salmon in the liquid not just until cold, but for something like 36 hours, during which time the flavour will mature. For me personally, the nicest way of cooking salmon is to confit it, to poach it very, very slowly in goose fat. We then serve it with sauce tapenade.

Turbot, monkfish, sea bass, skate, red mullet and tuna – even zander, a pike-perch – also feature at various times of the year on The Canteen menu, and the popularity of the smoked haddock with poached egg and new potatoes shows how simple things done well can still attract the paying customer. Most of these fish recipes involve little more than a quick pan-frying followed by a burst of heat in a hot oven.

TURBOT WITH BOULANGÈRE
LIE DE VIN

4 x 150 g (5 oz) pieces of turbot
2 large potatoes, peeled and finely sliced
50 ml (2 fl oz) goose fat
salt and freshly ground white pepper
1 large onion, peeled and finely sliced
200 g (7 oz) crépinette (pig's caul fat)
2 tablespoons olive oil
25 g (1 oz) unsalted butter
200 ml (7 fl oz) Fish Stock (SEE PAGE 192)

TO SERVE

1 recipe Sauce Lie de Vin (SEE PAGE 199)
24 cloves Confit of Garlic (SEE PAGE 207)

1. Preheat the oven to 180°C/350°F/Gas 4.
2. Wash the slices of potato to remove some of the starch, then dry. Heat the goose fat in a pan and poach the potatoes for 10 minutes or so, but avoid colouring them. Add salt and pepper while cooking. Drain well and leave to cool. Save the fat.
3. Cook the onion in exactly the same way as the potato. Drain and cool. Save the fat.
4. Season each piece of fish, and on to each place a layer of onion and a layer of potato.
5. Wash the *crépinette* well and squeeze out all the water. Spread it out on the work surface and make sure there are no holes or marbling in it. Cut into four pieces and wrap each piece around a fish piece plus topping. Roll over twice.
6. Heat the olive oil in a non-stick pan. Put in the four pieces of fish, potato and onion to the base, and add the butter. Colour to a nice golden brown, about 1½ minutes.
7. Line an ovenproof casserole dish with a large sheet of butter paper. Put in the fish, with the potato and onion to the top, pour in the stock and bring to the boil on top of the stove. then cook in the preheated oven for 7-10 minutes.
8. Meanwhile, heat and finish the sauce. Pan-fry the cloves of garlic in a dry pan to crisp them up.
9. To serve, arrange each plate with garlic cloves round the sides, with the fish in the centre, and the sauce around. This dish can be served with spinach, sauté potatoes, roasted potatoes or Savoy cabbage.

4 PORTIONS

4 x 150 g (5 oz) pieces of turbot
75 g (3 oz) unsalted butter
2 shallots, peeled and finely chopped
100 ml (3½ fl oz) white wine
750 ml (1¼ pints) Fish Stock (SEE PAGE 192)
1 teaspoon grain mustard
salt and freshly ground white pepper
2 tablespoons coarsely chopped flat parsley

ESCALOPE OF TURBOT POCHÉ

1. Melt 15 g (½ oz) of the butter in a large pan, and sweat the shallots to soften but not colour them.

2. Add the wine and reduce until virtually evaporated.

3. Add the stock and heat to 90°C/194°F. Place the fish carefully into it and cook for about 5 minutes, depending on thickness.

4. Remove 200 ml (7 fl oz) of the stock from the pan and into this whisk the rest of the butter. Mix in the mustard and some salt and pepper.

5. Add the chopped parsley to the fish still in the stock, and cook for 15 seconds. Drain the fish, the parsley still on top, and serve immediately.

CHEF'S NOTE

This is a supreme example of how easy many of our recipes are. If you have all the ingredients, you can have the dish ready in just over 5 minutes.

TRANCHENETTE
OF TURBOT
WITH GIROLLES
AND GARLIC

4 x 225 g (8 oz) pieces of turbot on the bone
225 g (8 oz) small girolles
50 g (2 oz) unsalted butter
50 g (2 oz) clarified butter

TO SERVE

24 cloves Confit of Garlic (SEE PAGE 207)
1 recipe Sauternes Sauce (SEE PAGE 200)

1.   Remove the stalks from the girolles, wash the heads thoroughly, and dry them carefully on kitchen cloth or kitchen paper without damaging them.

2.   Cook the girolles in the unsalted butter until golden brown.

3.   Heat the garlic cloves in a dry pan to crisp them up, and heat the sauce gently.

4.   Pan-fry the turbot in the hot clarified butter for 3-4 minutes on each side. When cooked, remove the dark skin from the fish.

5.   To serve, put a piece of fish on each plate, with the mushrooms and garlic cloves on top, and the sauce poured around.

4 PORTIONS

4 x 200 g (7 oz) pieces of monkfish on the bone
salt and freshly ground white pepper
100 ml (3½ fl oz) olive oil
1 recipe Tomato Sauce (SEE PAGE 204)

CASSOULETTE

450 g (1 lb) dry haricots blancs
300 ml (10 fl oz) goose fat
600 ml (1 pint) Fish Stock (SEE PAGE 192)
600 ml (1 pint) Chicken Stock (SEE PAGE 190)
2 slices Parma ham, not too thin, cut into julienne strips
3 plum tomatoes, chopped
2 shallots, peeled and chopped
1 garlic clove, peeled and crushed
2 tablespoons chopped flat parsley

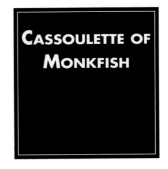

CASSOULETTE OF MONKFISH

1. Soak the beans in cold water for 24 hours, then drain well.
2. Quickly sweat the drained beans in 100 ml (3½ fl oz) of the goose fat in a suitable casserole. Add the fish stock and chicken stock, bring to the boil and simmer, covered, for 1½-2 hours until the beans are soft. Drain the beans, retaining the liquid, then reduce the liquid to a quarter of its original volume. Make sure the colour doesn't darken.
3. Add the ham julienne strips, tomato, shallot and garlic to the beans along with the reduced liquid, and cook for a further 10 minutes.
4. Season the fish, then pan-fry in the oil to a golden colour, about 6-7 minutes.
5. Meanwhile, add the parsley to the beans, stir in some more of the goose fat (for flavour, but make sure it's not too thin), and season.
6. Heat, but do not boil, the tomato sauce.
7. To serve, on each plate arrange a helping of beans with the fish on top. Pour the tomato sauce around.

CHEF'S NOTE

Haricot blancs can be bought from most supermarkets and delicatessens. This cassoulet of beans can be served with various fish, meats and sausages. If using it for meat, delete the fish stock and double the quantity of chicken stock.

ROAST MONKFISH WITH BRAISED SQUID,
FRESH NOODLES

4 PORTIONS

4 x 100 g (4 oz) fillets of monkfish
4 nice slices Parma ham
225 g (8 oz) squid, cut into julienne strips
85 ml (3 fl oz) olive oil
2 shallots, peeled and sliced
1 garlic clove, peeled and crushed
75 g (3 oz) unsalted butter
1 portion Red Wine Sauce *(SEE PAGE 195)*
20 g (¾ oz) flat parsley, chopped
2 tomatoes, skinned, seeded and cut into batons

TO SERVE

225 g (8 oz) Fresh Pasta *(SEE PAGE 215)*, cut into noodles
50 g (2 oz) unsalted butter
1 recipe Red Wine Sauce *(SEE PAGE 195)*

1. Wrap the monkfish in the ham and chill until ready to cook.
2. Pan-fry the squid strips in one-third of the olive oil in a very hot pan until golden brown. Drain the squid well and set aside.
3. Add another third of the oil to the pan, along with the shallot, garlic and butter. Pan-fry for a few minutes.
4. Return the squid to the pan along with the red wine sauce, and simmer to reduce right down to a thick consistency. Keep warm.
5. Pan-fry the ham-wrapped monkfish fillets in the remaining olive oil for about 6 minutes in a non-stick pan.
6. Heat the noodles up in an emulsion of the butter and a little water. Gently heat the sauce.
7. To serve, put the braised squid on the base of the plate. Cut the monkfish in half and place on the middle of the squid, place the noodles at the top of the plate, and pour the sauce around.

4 PORTIONS

4 x 700 g (1½ lb) skate wings
225 g (8 oz) Puff Pastry (SEE PAGE 215)
salt and freshly ground white pepper
2 egg yolks, beaten with a little salt

MOUSSE

3 fresh scallops   85 ml (3 fl oz) double cream
cayenne   1 large bunch watercress

TO SERVE

1 recipe Sauce Nantaise (SEE PAGE 204)
100 g (4 oz) mixed salad leaves
100 ml (3½ fl oz) Vinaigrette (SEE PAGE 206)
20 each of chervil and tarragon leaves and chive ends

CHASSON OF SKATE,
SAUCE NANTAISE, SALAD OF HERBS

1. Make the mousse first (up to 7 hours in advance, if chilled well). Purée the scallops, then fold in the cream. Season with a little salt and cayenne to taste.
2. Blanch the watercress in boiling salted water until just cooked, then refresh in cold water. Blend to a purée, and cool. When cold, mix into the scallop cream. Chill.
3. Roll the pastry out to 2-3 mm (⅛ in) thick, and cut into four circles, 13 x 15 cm (5-6 in) in diameter. Leave to chill for 30 minutes.
4. Preheat the oven to 180°C/350°F/Gas 4.
5. Blanch the skate wings in boiling water for 1 minute to help the flesh come off the bone. Drain and dry very thoroughly, then remove the bones.
6. Cut each wing in half and you will have eight pieces of fillet, four of them larger than the other four. Take the larger pieces and cover them with equal quantities of the mousse. Place the smaller fillets on top to completely cover the mousse – you don't want the moistness of the mousse to touch the pastry at all - and mould in your hand to a small pillow shape.
7. Season the skate pillows with salt and pepper, and place each on one-half of each of the pastry circles. Egg wash around the edges of the pastry circles, and bring the other half over the skate to form a pasty or turnover shape. Press the joins together, then close securely by crimping or by cutting along the inside of the half-moon shape. Egg wash the outsides of the little pasties, and place on a baking sheet.
8. Bake the pasties in the well preheated oven for 10 minutes. Bring out of the oven and allow to rest for about 5 minutes. Meanwhile, warm the sauce through gently.
9. To serve, place the pasty on a warm, not hot, plate with the dressed salad leaves at the top and the sauce to the side. Scatter the herbs on top of the salad.

4 PORTIONS

4 x 450 g (1 lb) skate wings
100 ml (3½ fl oz) vegetable oil
25 g (1 oz) white peppercorns, crushed
salt and freshly ground white pepper
25 g (1 oz) unsalted butter

TO SERVE

24 baby leeks
25 g (1 oz) unsalted butter
1 recipe Sauce Lie de Vin (SEE PAGE 199)

**SKATE AU
POIVRE,**
*SAUCE
LIE DE VIN*

1. Trim off the knuckle of the skate, and cut around the outside with a pair of scissors to remove the skirt.

2. Heat a non-stick pan (or pans) with the vegetable oil. Pass the skate wings through the peppercorns, to get a good coating on both sides. Season with salt and pan-fry in the oil. This will take approximately 10 minutes, depending upon the thickness of the wings. Halfway through cooking, add the butter, which will help the browning. The skate will need to be turned for 2 or 3 minutes before it is ready.

3. Meanwhile, trim the leeks. Cook in boiling salted water until nearly tender. Whilst hot, cut into 4 cm (1½ in) lozenges. Melt the butter in a pan, gently toss the leeks in it, and season with salt and pepper.

4. Heat the sauce through gently.

5. To serve, place the leeks at the top of the plate and the skate below them. Put a small ring of sauce around

CHEF'S NOTE

*A*lways cook skate on the bone: the fish cooks better, the flesh doesn't shrink, it retains moisture and is tender and full of flavour.

DAURADE ROYALE BARIGOULE, *Sauce Vierge*

4 PORTIONS

*4 x 175 g (6 oz) fillets of daurade royale
(red sea bream)
4 Artichokes Barigoule (SEE PAGE 210)
100 ml (3½ fl oz) olive oil*

TO SERVE

*1 recipe Sauce Vierge (SEE PAGE 205)
4 sprigs each of fresh chervil and tarragon
20 chive ends*

1. Heat the artichokes and their liquor in a pan.
2. Heat the olive oil in a non-stick frying pan, and cook the fish fillets rapidly for about 1½ minutes on each side until golden brown.
3. Make the sauce, and slice the artichokes thinly.
4. To serve, place the artichoke pieces down the centre of each plate, place the fish on top, and the rest of the barigoule and liquor on the fish. Pour the sauce around the plate, and garnish with the chervil, tarragon and chives.

4 PORTIONS

4 x 175 g (6 oz) fillets of sea bass
Dijon mustard
2 tablespoons Mushroom Duxelles (SEE PAGE 215)
2 tablespoons Tomato Fondue (SEE PAGE 206)
1 recipe Soft Herb Crust (SEE PAGE 214)
400 ml (14 fl oz) Fish Stock (SEE PAGE 192)
100 ml (3½ fl oz) olive oil
200 ml (7 fl oz) white wine

TO SERVE

1 recipe White Wine Cream Sauce (SEE PAGE 200)
100 ml (3½ fl oz) double cream, semi-whipped
salt and freshly ground white pepper
4 tablespoons finely snipped chives

ESCALOPE OF SEA BASS WITH A SOFT PARSLEY CRUST, *CRÈME LÉGÈRE WITH CHIVES*

1. Preheat the oven to 200°C/400°F/Gas 6.
2. Smear each piece of fish lightly with mustard. Then add layers of duxelles, fondue and soft herb crust.
3. Line a casserole with butter paper. Put in the fish, and enough stock, oil and wine, mixed together, to cover the fish *but not the topping*. Bring to the boil on top of the stove, then place in the preheated oven for 5-7 minutes.
4. Heat the sauce gently, add the cream, and blend quickly with a hand blender. Season, then add the chives at the last moment.
5. To serve, put an escalope of fish on each plate with sauce around it. Good accompaniments are noodles or spinach.

CHEF'S NOTE

Sea bass is delicate, but so is this soft parsley crust, and they work well together. Apart from the complementary flavours, the texture is beautiful in the mouth.

ROAST JOHN DORY WITH ENDIVE
AND SABAYON OF TARRAGON

8 x 75 g (3 oz) fillets of John Dory, skinned
salt and freshly ground white pepper
100 ml (3½ fl oz) olive oil
4 medium heads Belgian endive (chicory)
50 g (2 oz) butter

TO SERVE

1 recipe Velouté for Fish (SEE PAGE 198)
50 ml (2 fl oz) double cream, whipped
50 g (2 oz) tarragon leaves

1. Season the John Dory fillets and pan-fry in the olive oil in a non-stick pan for approximately 3-4 minutes altogether.

2. Separate the endive leaves and cut into long batons, about the thickness of your little finger. Blanch in boiling salted water for 1 minute. Drain well, then gently sauté and colour in the butter.

3. Heat the velouté to reduce it slightly, then add the whipped cream. Whisk for approximately 2 minutes with a hand blender, then place back on the heat. Add the tarragon.

4. To serve, put the endive in the centre of the plate, the fish on top, and the sabayon of tarragon around.

CHEF'S NOTE

You must be careful with John Dory, because it is staggering how quickly it cooks. If you turn your back for a second, it can easily overcook.

4 PORTIONS

4 x 175 g (6 oz) pieces of cod
about 150 ml (5 fl oz) olive oil
25 g (1 oz) curry powder

TO SERVE

36 tiny sprigs thyme
vegetable oil for deep-frying
175 g (6 oz) small girolles
25 g (1 oz) unsalted butter
salt
30 cloves Confit of Garlic (SEE PAGE 207)
1 recipe Sauternes Sauce (SEE PAGE 200)

ROAST CURRIED COD
WITH GIROLLES AND CONFIT OF GARLIC

1. Deep-fry the sprigs of thyme in hot oil for a few seconds, then leave to drain on absorbent kitchen paper. They should be crisp. This can be done about 10-20 minutes in advance.

2. Mix 50 ml (2 fl oz) of the olive oil with the curry powder to make a thin paste. Brush this generously over the cod.

3. Preheat a non-stick frying pan and pan-fry the cod in the remaining olive oil for 7-8 minutes.

4. Pan-fry the girolles in the butter until golden brown. Season with a little salt.

5. Fry the confit of garlic in a dry pan to crisp it up.

6. Heat the sauce through gently.

7. To serve, place the cod in the centre of the plate and arrange the girolles, garlic and thyme neatly over and around. Pour the sauce around the garnish.

LASAGNE OF COD
WITH TAPENADE

4 PORTIONS

4 x 225 g (8 oz) fillets of cod
4 tablespoons Tapenade (SEE PAGE 206)
½ recipe Fresh Pasta, cut into 16 sheets lasagne,
7.5 cm (3 in) square, cooked (SEE PAGE 215)
15 g (½ oz) unsalted butter
salt

SAUCE

200 ml (7 fl oz) Fish Stock (SEE PAGE 192)
75 g (3 oz) unsalted butter
1 teaspoon double cream
48 tarragon leaves
lemon juice

1. Steam the fish above boiling water until cooked, about 6 minutes.

2. Flake the flesh into a warm bowl, and lightly mix in the tapenade. Keep warm.

3. Reheat the pasta in the butter with a little water and some salt. Drain well. Arrange on each plate seven alternating layers of pasta and fish, pasta first and last.

4. Bring the fish stock to the boil, then whisk in the butter and stabilise with the cream. Add the tarragon and infuse for 30 seconds. Add a little lemon juice to heighten the flavour.

5. To serve, pour the sauce around the fish, making sure the tarragon is evenly divided, and spoon ½ tablespoon on the top of each lasagne to give the pasta a nice shine.

CHEF'S NOTE

One of the problems of being a chef is that you sometimes have to do things that are not strictly necessary in order to impress or to appear creative. A piece of cod spread with tapenade and served with noodles would be just as nice as the above!

4 PORTIONS

4 x 150 g (5 oz) pieces of cod fillet
sea salt and freshly ground white pepper
4 teaspoons Dijon mustard
4 teaspoons Tomato Fondue (SEE PAGE 206)
4 teaspoons Mushroom Duxelles (SEE PAGE 215)
200 g (7 oz) Soft Herb Crust (SEE PAGE 214)
400 ml (14 fl oz) white wine
400 ml (14 fl oz) Fish Stock (SEE PAGE 192)
olive oil
lemon juice

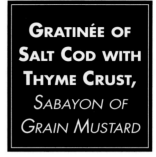

GRATINÉE OF SALT COD WITH THYME CRUST, SABAYON OF GRAIN MUSTARD

TO SERVE

1 recipe Sabayon of Grain Mustard (SEE PAGE 199)

1. Place the pieces of cod in a tray and sprinkle with a little sea salt - slightly more than you would use if seasoning ordinarily. Cover with cling film and leave in the fridge for a day. The salt will draw the liquids out.
2. Preheat the oven to 220°C/425°F/Gas 7.
3. Drain and dry the pieces of salt cod on pieces of kitchen paper, and season with some pepper. Lightly spread the top of each piece with Dijon mustard, then the tomato fondue, then the mushroom duxelles.
4. Top all this with the soft herb crust, then place on a butter paper in a shallow ovenproof dish.
5. Add the white wine, fish stock and a splash of olive oil to the pan, enough to cover the fish, *but not the topping*. Season this cooking liquid with salt and pepper and a little lemon juice.
6. Bring to the boil on top of the stove, then cook in the preheated oven for about 5 minutes.
7. Meanwhile, make the sabayon.
8. To serve, place the drained cod on a warm plate and pour the sauce around. Place under a preheated grill until the crust and sauce are a golden brown colour. This should take approximately 1 minute. Serve with fresh noodles if you like.

SMOKED HADDOCK WITH POACHED EGG AND NEW POTATOES

4 PORTIONS

4 x 200 g (7 oz) pieces of naturally smoked haddock
warm milk to cover
salt and freshly ground white pepper

TO SERVE

1 recipe Mustard Beurre Blanc (SEE PAGE 203)
20 medium new potatoes
4 teaspoons white wine vinegar
4 eggs
4 sprigs chervil

1. Make the mustard beurre blanc and keep warm.
2. Cook the new potatoes in boiling salted water until tender. Slice and season. Keep warm.
3. Place the fish into a shallow pan and cover with warm milk. Cook for about 5 minutes, or until the skin peels off easily, then remove from the milk and take off and discard any skin (and any bones). Keep warm.
4. Bring a small pan of water to the boil, then add the vinegar and gently poach the eggs (SEE PAGE 30).
5. To serve, make a bed of sliced potatoes for the fish, then place the egg on top of the fish. Garnish with chervil.

4 PORTIONS

4 x 175 g (6 oz) pieces of zander
salt and freshly ground white pepper
50 ml (2 fl oz) olive oil

CHOUCROÛTE

450 g (1 lb) cooked choucroûte
1 continental garlic sausage
50 g (2 oz) green back bacon
4 small carrots
1 bouquet garni   20 juniper berries
Fish Stock (SEE PAGE 192)
back fat (skin off the back bacon)

TO SERVE

1 recipe Juniper Berry Butter Sauce (SEE PAGE 201)

ROAST ZANDER WITH CHOUCROÛTE, JUNIPER BERRY BUTTER SAUCE

1. Heat the oven to 140-150°C/275-300°F/Gas 1-2.
2. For the choucroûte, in a heavy-bottomed casserole, put the choucroûte, sausage, bacon, carrots, bouquet garni and juniper berries. Half cover with fish stock, and lay the back fat on top. Bring to the boil on the stove, then cook in the preheated oven for about 40 minutes. Remove the sausage after 25 minutes, as it will be cooked. Keep warm.
3. Season the fish and pan-fry in a little olive oil in a hot non-stick pan for 2½ minutes on each side.
4. Slice the sausage. Remove the bacon and bouquet garni, and lightly mix the sausage and choucroûte together.
5. To serve, on each plate arrange a helping of choucroûte and sausage, with sliced carrot, some bacon if liked, and the fish on top. Pour the sauce around.

CHEF'S NOTE

If zander (a freshwater fish which is a cross between a pike and a perch) is unobtainable, the recipe works very well with sea bass, sea bream or wild salmon. The sausage we use at The Canteen is Saucisse de Morteau, which comes from La Bresse area of France.

Choucroûte can be bought tinned from delicatessens, either raw or pre-cooked.

85

FRESH SALMON, POMME SAUTÉ, TRUFFLE-INFUSED CABBAGE CREAM

4 PORTIONS

4 x 150 g (5 oz) supremes of fresh salmon
500 ml (17 fl oz) Chicken Stock (SEE PAGE 190)
200 g (7 oz) smoked belly pork
3 large Savoy cabbage leaves (outside ones
are the best), washed
salt and freshly ground white pepper
300 ml (10 fl oz) double cream
truffle oil   100 ml (3½ fl oz) olive oil

TO SERVE

1 recipe Pomme Sauté (SEE PAGE 209)
100 g (4 oz) seasonal salad leaves
16 each of chive ends and chervil sprigs

1.   Place the chicken stock in a pan, add the smoked belly pork, and bring to the boil. Remove from the heat and allow to infuse. The pork can be left in the stock until it is cold. Remove the pork from the stock, and use for something else.
2.   Cook the outside leaves of the cabbage in boiling salted water until completely soft, then refresh using iced water. Strain off and liquidise to a purée.
3.   Meanwhile sauté the potatoes.
4.   Place the infused chicken stock in a pan, and boil to reduce by about one-third. Taste to see how smoky it is. Add the cream and reduce to a coating consistency.
5.   Add the cabbage purée and a little truffle oil, then season and remove from the heat.
6.   Sauté the salmon in the olive oil until pink, about 3-4 minutes on the skin side to crisp it, 1½ minutes on the other side.
7.   To serve, place the sauté potatoes on the plate with the cooked salmon on top, then arrange the seasonal salad leaves on top of that. Scatter on some chives and chervil. Pour the cabbage cream sauce around the potatoes.

CHEF'S NOTE

As far as the relative merits of farmed and wild salmon go, it can't be denied that the best are young spring salmon from the rivers, caught when the water is still cold. When you get a fish in April or May, fresh from the sea, still with sea lice on it, it's fantastic.

SALMON CONFIT
WITH SAUCE TAPENADE

4 PORTIONS

4 x 150 g (5 oz) escalopes of salmon
1.2 litres (2 pints) goose fat
fleur de sel (see below)

TO SERVE

1 recipe Sauce Tapenade (SEE PAGE 199)

1. Using a pan in which the goose fat is about 7.5 cm (3 in) deep, heat the fat to 45-50°C (113-122°F), and poach the salmon for about 4 or 5 minutes.
2. Drain well and season the salmon with the salt.
3. Heat the sauce and serve with the fish.

CHEF'S NOTE

Fleur de sel is an undried and untreated sea salt. If you can't find it in delicatessens, use ordinary sea salt instead. This dish is good accompanied by Ratatouille (see page 212).

4 PORTIONS

4 x 150 g (5 oz) pieces of salmon
1 good-sized heart of Savoy cabbage
salt and freshly ground white pepper
1-2 smoked bacon rinds
40 g (1½ oz) unsalted butter
8 slices ventreche ham (or very finely sliced streaky bacon)

TO SERVE

1 recipe Sauce Lie de Vin (SEE PAGE 199)

1. Blanch the cabbage in boiling, salted water with the smoked bacon rinds, and cook for 2 minutes. Drain well, remove the rinds, add the butter, and season.
2. Grill the salmon under a preheated grill for 1½ minutes on each side.
3. At the same time, cook the ham lightly under the grill, without colouring it.
4. Meanwhile, heat the sauce through gently.
5. To serve, drain the cabbage again, and place some in the centre of each plate. Put the salmon on top of the cabbage and the ham on top of the salmon. Pour the sauce around.

CHEF'S NOTE

We use ventreche ham, a dried and cured bacon from the belly. This is very finely sliced, so it crisps very rapidly. It does not contain any water. Substitute any good British or continental bacon, so long as it shares the same qualities.

GRILLED DARNE OF SALMON

WITH ASPARAGUS, NEW POTATOES, SAUCE MOUSSELINE

4 x 200 g (7 oz) darnes of salmon, scaled
200 ml (7 fl oz) olive oil
salt and freshly ground white pepper

TO SERVE

28 asparagus tips
28 new potatoes, peeled and turned
1 cucumber, cut into 28 turned barrel shapes
50 g (2 oz) unsalted butter
25 g (1 oz) dill, chopped
1 recipe Sauce Mousseline (SEE PAGE 203)

1. Peel and cook the asparagus in boiling, salted water, then refresh in cold water. Cook the potatoes in the same way, but until tender. Only blanch the cucumber pieces momentarily.

2. Coat the darnes of salmon generously with the olive oil, and season with salt and pepper. Cook on a red-hot, ridged cast-iron pan, or under a red-hot grill for approximately 4 minutes on each side, depending on size.

3. Reheat the vegetables separately in an emulsion of the butter and a little water.

4. Add the dill to the cucumber and season.

5. To serve, put the darne on the plate, and arrange the potatoes and asparagus to the sides, the cucumber on top. Serve the warm sauce on the side of the plate.

4 PORTIONS

4 x 275 g (10 oz) red mullet, scaled, filleted and
pin-boned
salt and fresh ground white pepper
2 tablespoons olive oil

TO SERVE

12 baby fennel, trimmed
8 Beignets of Sage (SEE PAGE 213)
1 recipe Sauce Vierge (SEE PAGE 205)
15-20 stoned black olives, halved
a handful each of chervil, tarragon and chives

RED MULLET
WITH BEIGNETS
OF SAGE,
SAUCE VIERGE

1. Blanch the baby fennel in boiling salted water. Drain well and keep warm.
2. Make the beignets of sage and keep warm.
3. Meanwhile, seaon then pan-fry the fish in the olive oil in a large non-stick pan for about 1½ minutes on each side.
4. Quickly finish the sauce, adding the tomato dice at the very last moment, along with the olives.
5. Arrange the fish, 2 fillets per plate, with the beignets of sage on top. Spoon the sauce around, and decorate with the fennel and herbs.

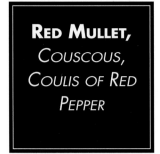

RED MULLET, COUSCOUS, COULIS OF RED PEPPER

4 PORTIONS

*4 x 225 g (8 oz) red mullet, scaled, filleted and
pin-boned
salt and freshly ground white pepper
about 25 g (1 oz) plain flour
100 ml (3½ fl oz) olive oil*

RED PEPPER COULIS

*3 red peppers
50 ml (2 fl oz) olive oil
50 g (2 oz) unsalted butter*

TO SERVE

*1 recipe Couscous (SEE PAGE 212)
20 basil leaves
vegetable oil for deep-frying*

1. For the coulis, skin the peppers, then cut them in half and remove the seeds. Place the majority of the flesh into a processor and blend to a purée. Add the olive oil and butter and blend again, then pass through a fine strainer. Chop the remaining red pepper into tiny dice, and add to the coulis.

2. Start to heat through the couscous, and deep-fry the basil leaves in the hot oil. The oil temperature must be no more than 130°C/266°F in order to keep the leaves green; if hotter than that, the leaves will turn brown. Drain on kitchen paper and keep warm.

3. To cook the fish, coat the fillets in seasoned flour, then pan-fry them in most of the olive oil until cooked - for about 4 minutes or so on the skin side, 1 minute on the other.

4. To serve, place the couscous into a ring mould and press down on each plate. Place two mullet fillets on top, brush with olive oil, then garnish with the basil leaves.

CHEF'S NOTE

This is easy eating, ideal for when you're not really very hungry. The couscous absorbs the sauce, and it can all be eaten with a fork.

4 PORTIONS

4 x 175 g (6 oz) supremes of tuna
500 ml (17 fl oz) olive oil
salt and freshly ground white pepper

PIPÉRADE

1 medium onion, peeled
3 red peppers, skinned and seeded
6 plum tomatoes, skinned and seeded
50 ml (2 fl oz) good olive oil
1 garlic clove, peeled and crushed
1 bay leaf
1 sprig thyme

TO SERVE

2 heads frisée endive
12 tarragon leaves
20 each of chive ends and chervil sprigs
25 ml (1 fl oz) white wine vinegar
150 ml (5 fl oz) good olive oil
100 ml (3½ fl oz) balsamic vinegar

CONFIT OF TUNA,
PIPÉRADE, BALSAMIC DRESSING

1.   For the pipérade, cut the onion, pepper and tomato into batons about the thickness of your little finger. Put the olive oil into a heavy pan and sweat off the onion and garlic until soft, then add the red pepper, bay leaf and thyme, and season with salt and pepper. When the pepper is soft, add the tomato, and cook for a further 2 minutes. Season again if necessary. Remove the bay and thyme.

2.   Use the yellow centre parts of the frisée endive only. Wash and dry well. Mix with the herbs and store in a cool place.

3.   Put the white wine vinegar in a bowl and whisk in 85 ml (3 fl oz) of the olive oil to make a dressing.

4.   Heat the cooking olive oil to 60°C/140°F, and submerge the tuna in it. The tuna will take approximately 8 minutes (depending on thickness) to cook to nice and pink in the middle.

5.   To serve, place the pipérade in the centre of the plate, and the tuna on top. Toss the salad in the dressing, season and place a neat ball on top of the tuna. Spoon the remaining olive oil and the balsamic vinegar around the tuna.

GRILLED TUNA,
RATATOUILLE, TAPENADE, BEURRE DE TOMATE

4 PORTIONS

4 x 150 g (5 oz) pieces yellow fin tuna
4 teaspoons Tapenade (SEE PAGE 206)

BEURRE DE TOMATE

225 g (8 oz) cherry tomatoes
2 teaspoons olive oil
50 g (2 oz) unsalted butter
salt and freshly ground white pepper

TO SERVE

1 recipe Ratatouille (SEE PAGE 212)

1.   To make the beurre de tomate, liquidise the cherry tomatoes, and pass them through a fine plastic sieve.

2.   Heat the tomato pulp in a pan, but keep it below boiling point. Whisk in the olive oil, butter and seasoning.

3.   Grill the tuna on each side for 1½ minutes to medium. Then spread the tapenade evenly over the upper surface.

4.   Warm the ratatouille through gently.

5.   To serve, put the ratatouille at the top of the plate, and the tuna with the beurre de tomate around it at the front.

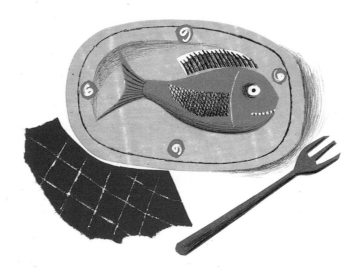

ROAST TUNA,
AUBERGINE CAVIAR, SAUCE AIGRE-DOUX

4 PORTIONS

4 x 175 g (6 oz) slices of tuna
salt and freshly ground white pepper
100 ml (3½ fl oz) olive oil

TO SERVE

1 recipe Sauce Aigre-doux (SEE PAGE 197)
2 recipes Aubergine Caviar (SEE PAGE 211)
20 cloves Confit of Garlic (SEE PAGE 207)
4 sprigs chervil

1. Warm through the sauce and the aubergine caviar, and fry the garlic cloves in a dry pan to crisp them.
2. Season the tuna and pan-fry in the oil for about 5 minutes altogether. Drain well.
3. To serve, place the aubergine caviar on the plate and the tuna on top. Pour the sauce around, place the garlic cloves on top, and garnish finally with the chervil.

MEAT, POULTRY & GAME

MEAT, POULTRY & GAME

AS MAIN COURSES, meat, poultry and game obviously take a little longer to cook than fish dishes, but the recipes here are not complicated when transferred to a domestic context. You must perhaps plan ahead a little more, and start work a little earlier. The techniques involved too are very straightforward, principally pan-frying or grilling for smaller pieces, roasting for larger joints or for birds. There are a few recipes which involve poaching and braising.

I like to roast poultry, whether domestic or game birds, and if you follow the recipes here, you can perfect the technique of roasting a chicken, a quail, a grouse, woodcock or pigeon. Then you can ring the changes on accompaniments and sauces, and I've given quite a few ideas. The secret is to seal and then roast hot and quick. Often I poach a chicken first and *then* roast it; the poaching partially cooks it but releases the fat, allowing the skin to caramelise during the roasting. Another favourite poultry dish is confit of duck – duck legs poached in goose fat – and I give a couple of ideas of how to serve it. Grouse is a seasonal treat (as are many game birds) and at The Canteen we like to serve it in the traditional way, with all the proper garnishes.

Roast joints are a favourite of the domestic cook, and we often have a roast of some sort on the menu. Some are simpler, such as rump or best end of lamb, others are more complicated, such as the stuffed lamb saddle recipes, or the roast suckling pig (an occasional special at The Canteen). One way of making a number of these recipes more manageable at home is to ask your butcher to bone the joints and prepare the basics for you; if he's worth his salt, he'll be willing to do this, and happy to utilise his skills.

We also offer a number of steak recipes, and, as with the poached egg and smoked haddock recipe, a constant favourite is the simplest one, a steak served with béarnaise sauce! The braised oxtail *en crépinette* may be more complicated, but it earns its place here because it has been on The Canteen menu every year since we opened.

ROAST CHICKEN WITH HERBS, POMME FONDANT, JUS RÔTI

4 PORTIONS

2 x 1.35 kg (3 lb) chickens
salt and freshly ground white pepper
100 ml (3½ fl oz) vegetable oil

HERB FARCE

100 g (4 oz) unsalted butter
100 g (4 oz) chopped parsley
40 g (1½ oz) breadcrumbs

TO SERVE

24 baby leeks, trimmed   25 g (1 oz) unsalted butter
16 small banana-shaped Pomme Fondant (SEE PAGE 208)
½ recipe Jus Rôti (SEE PAGE 195)
12 cloves Confit of Garlic (SEE PAGE 207)
20 g (¾ oz) each of coarsely chopped chervil, tarragon
and chives

1. Preheat the oven to 200°C/400°F/Gas 6.
2. For the herb farce, mix all the ingredients together, and season with salt and pepper. Place in a piping bag.
3. Remove the legs, wings, neck and wishbones from the chicken. Pipe the farce between the skin and flesh of the breasts, and smooth out evenly.
4. Season the chickens and seal carefully in a hot pan in the oil. Roast in the preheated oven for approximately 25 minutes. Allow to rest for 10 minutes before carefully removing the breasts from the bone.
5. Blanch the leeks in boiling water, and cut into 5 cm (2 in) pieces. Reheat in an emulsion of the butter and a little water.
6. Heat through the potatoes, and the sauce. Fry the garlic cloves in a dry pan to crisp them up.
7. To serve, place a chicken breast at the bottom of the plate, and the leeks, potatoes and garlic at the top. Put the chopped herbs into the sauce and pour this around.

4 PORTIONS

8 x 100-150 g (4-5 oz) quails
25 ml (1 fl oz) goose fat
24-32 slices ventreche ham (or very finely sliced streaky bacon)
24 nice sage leaves
100 ml (3½ fl oz) vegetable oil

TO SERVE

1 recipe Braised Cabbage (SEE PAGE 209)
½ recipe Jus Rôti (SEE PAGE 195)
8 cloves Confit of Garlic (SEE PAGE 207)

ROAST QUAIL WITH SAGE, BRAISED WHITE CABBAGE, JUS RÔTI

1. Preheat the oven to 200°C/400°F/Gas 6.
2. Paint the quails with some of the goose fat, then alternate 3-4 ham slices with 3 sage leaves across the breasts of each bird, tucking firmly in at the bottom. Repaint with goose fat, then tie to secure.
3. Roast in the vegetable oil in the preheated oven for 8-10 minutes, then allow to rest for 2 minutes.
4. Meanwhile, heat the cabbage and sauce through gently. Fry the garlic in a dry pan to crisp it up.
5. To serve, place 2 quails on each plate beside the cabbage, then add the garlic. Pour the sauce over and around.

CHEF'S NOTE

You should only buy French quails, as they have so much more flavour than their English equivalent. The French have always been the masters of poultry breeding, and we should follow their example in this country.

ROAST QUAIL, VENTRECHE HAM, BRAISED CABBAGE, BRIOCHE DUMPLINGS, MADEIRA SAUCE

4 PORTIONS

4 x 175-225 g (6-8 oz) quails
25 ml (1 fl oz) goose fat
4 slices back bacon
100 ml (3½ fl oz) vegetable oil

TO SERVE

6 large carrots
salt
1 very small white cabbage
600 ml (1 pint) Chicken Stock (SEE PAGE 190)
15 g (½ oz) unsalted butter
8 Brioche Dumplings (SEE PAGE 218)
12 slices ventreche ham (or very finely sliced streaky bacon)
1 recipe Madeira Sauce (SEE PAGE 194)

1.   Preheat the oven to 200°C/400°F/Gas 6.
2.   Paint the birds with a little of the goose fat, then cover the breasts with a protective slice of back bacon. Paint again with goose fat and tie to secure.
3.   Roast in the vegetable oil in the preheated oven for 12-14 minutes, then allow to rest for 5 minutes.
4.   Meanwhile, top and tail the carrots, then cut into 12 nice even pieces, using an apple corer. Cook in lightly boiling salted water until still just crisp.
5.   Break the cabbage into rough pieces, blanch in boiling salted water, then drain. Braise in 50 ml (2 fl oz) of the chicken stock with the butter for about 5 minutes, or until tender. Reheat the carrots in this at the last minute.
6.   Braise the dumplings in the remaining chicken stock for 3-4 minutes, then drain.
7.   Grill the ham or bacon at the last minute, and heat the sauce.
8.   To serve, place the cabbage in the centre of the plate, the carrots at one side and the ham at the other. Place the bird on the cabbage and the dumplings at the top of the plate. Pour the sauce over the bird and the cabbage.

4 PORTIONS

4 x 175-200 g (6-7 oz) magrets (duck breasts)
175 g (6 oz) puréed black olives (keep the stones)
25 ml (1 fl oz) goose fat
salt and freshly ground white pepper

CREAMED CABBAGE

1 Savoy cabbage   1 large carrot
50 g (2 oz) peeled celeriac
50 g (2 oz) smoked streaky bacon, cut into lardons
50 ml (2 fl oz) goose fat
100 ml (3½ fl oz) double cream

TO SERVE

1 recipe Red Wine Sauce (SEE PAGE 195)
2 tablespoons double cream
25 g (1 oz) hard unsalted butter, diced

MAGRET OF DUCK WITH BLACK OLIVES

1.   Preheat the oven to 220°C/425°F/Gas 7.
2.   Chill the duck breasts well, and then remove some of the excess fat with a sharp knife. Make a slight incision using a sharp thin knife, and form a pocket between the fat and flesh. Place the puréed olives in a piping bag and lightly fill the pocket on each breast. Do not over fill, as it will begin to run out when cooked. Chill until ready to cook.
3.   To cook the cabbage, discard the outer leaves, and cut the remainder into baton-sized strips. Peel the carrot, and cut it and the celeriac into thick julienne strips.
4.   In a good-sized, heavy-bottomed pan, heat a third of the goose fat and sauté the lardons of bacon. When they start to colour, add the carrot and celeriac, cook for a few minutes, then drain into a colander.
5.   Place the pan back on the heat, add half of the remaining goose fat, and cook the cabbage in it for a few minutes. Remove and add to the bacon, carrot and celeriac.
6.   Pan-fry the duck in the goose fat, sealing it on both sides, and then cook on the skin side for 5 minutes in the preheated oven. Remove and allow to rest for 5 minutes.
7.   Meanwhile, put half the sauce into a small pan, add the olive stones, and gently reduce by about half. Add the rest of the sauce, the cream and the butter. Sieve.
8.   Reheat the cabbage in the remaining goose fat and season to taste. Pour in the double cream, and reduce lightly just to coat.
9.   To serve, place the cabbage at the top of the plate. Arrange the duck, either whole or sliced thinly, below the cabbage, and pour the sauce around.

CONFIT DE CANARD

WITH CEPS AND TRUFFLE, MADEIRA SAUCE

4 PORTIONS

4 large or 8 small duck legs
25 g (1 oz) sel rose
25 g (1 oz) rock salt
2 garlic cloves, peeled
4 sprigs thyme
2 bay leaves
1.5 litres (2½ pints) goose fat
4 shallots, peeled and sliced

TO SERVE

200 g (7 oz) fresh ceps
25 g (1 oz) unsalted butter
25 g (1 oz) fresh truffle, cleaned and diced
1 recipe Madeira Sauce (SEE PAGE 194)
1 recipe Pomme Fondant (SEE PAGE 208)

1. Marinate the duck legs for 12 hours with the two salts, 1 crushed garlic clove, 2 sprigs thyme and 1 bay leaf. This draws the blood out of the legs.

2. Wipe the marinade off, dry well, and place the legs in the warm goose fat. Add the remaining garlic, thyme and bay leaf, and the shallots. Braise on top of the stove very gently for about 1¼ hours. The heat must not exceed 70°C/158°F; if it gets too hot, add a little water. The legs are ready when the thigh bones are very loose. Remove these if you like.

3. To store, if not using straightaway, strain the goose fat, discarding the vegetables and herbs, and pour enough fat over the duck legs in a suitable container to cover them completely and make them airtight. Chill.

4. When you wish to cook and serve, preheat the oven to 200-220°C/400-425°F/Gas 6-7.

5. Clean and wash the ceps, and slice not too thinly into cross sections. Sauté them in the butter, then add about half of the diced truffle at the last minute.

6. Heat the sauce gently, and add the remaining truffle at the last minute. Heat through the potatoes.

7. Remove the duck legs from their covering of goose fat, scrape off excess fat, and pan-fry the legs in a dry non-stick pan for a few minutes. Place them in the preheated oven for about 8-12 minutes, depending on the size of the legs. Watch that the bone doesn't turn black.

8. To serve, put the ceps on the plate, and the duck leg(s) on top. Place the potato to one side and pour the sauce over the duck.

4 PORTIONS

4 large or 8 small duck legs
12-24 cloves
25 g (1 oz) sel rose
25 g (1 oz) rock salt
2 garlic cloves, peeled
4 sprigs thyme
2 bay leaves
1.5 litres (2½ pints) goose fat
4 shallots, peeled and sliced
50 g (2 oz) liquid honey
juice of 1 lemon
100 ml (3½ fl oz) good quality olive oil

TO SERVE

1 recipe Braised Cabbage (SEE PAGE 209)
1 recipe Pomme Anna (SEE PAGE 208)
1 recipe Bittersweet Port Wine Sauce (SEE PAGE 197)

CONFIT DE CANARD WITH HONEY AND CLOVES, BITTERSWEET PORT WINE SAUCE

1.   Confit the duck legs in exactly the same way as in the last recipe (steps 1-3), but before doing so, stud each leg with 3 cloves.
2.   When you wish to cook and serve, preheat the oven to 200°C/400°F/Gas 6.
3.   Remove the duck legs from their covering of goose fat, scrape off excess fat, and pan-fry the legs in a dry non-stick pan for a few minutes. Coat with the mixed honey, lemon juice and olive oil then roast them in this mixture in the preheated oven for 8-12 minutes, depending on the size of the legs. Baste so that the flavours penetrate the flesh.
4.   Heat up the cabbage, potatoes and sauce.
5.   To serve, put the cabbage in the centre of the plate and the duck leg(s) on top. Place the potato to the side and the sauce around.

CHEF'S NOTE

The amount of goose fat needed to confit these duck legs may seem a lot, but it can be used over and over again. In fact, after it has been used to confit duck, its flavour is even better! The confit can be prepared about 2 weeks before eating, and should be done at least 4-5 days in advance for the flavours to mature.

ROAST BREAST OF GOOSNARGH DUCK
WITH ELDERBERRIES

4 PORTIONS

2 x 1.8 kg (4 lb) ducks
salt and freshly ground white pepper
1 tablespoon vegetable oil

TO SERVE

1 recipe Lentilles du Pays (SEE PAGE 212)
1 recipe Red Wine Sauce (SEE PAGE 195)
25 g (1 oz) elderberries, washed

1. Preheat the oven to 200°C/400°F/Gas 6.
2. Clean the ducks, and remove all excess fat, the wishbones, the legs, wings and the bottom of the carcasses. (Use these in stocks or in confit, etc.)
3. Blanch the duck breasts in boiling salted water for 2-3 minutes. This removes the little fatty bits, and helps the duck skin to go crisp. Dry well.
4. Seal the breasts in a pan in the oil, then roast in the oil in the preheated oven, breast side down, for about 10-15 minutes.
5. Remove from the pan and allow to rest for 5 minutes, before taking the breasts carefully off the bone. Trim carefully with scissors to remove any excess fat.
6. Place the breasts in a hot, dry, non-stick pan, skin side down, to crisp the fat, about 1½-2 minutes.
7. Meanwhile, warm through the lentils and the sauce. Add the elderberries to the sauce some 30 seconds or so before serving.
8. To serve, put the lentils in the middle of the plate. Slice the duck nicely and place on top. Pour the sauce over and around.

CHEF'S NOTE
You need to have the duck breasts on the bone for this dish, so buy whole ducks, and confit the legs as in the recipes on pages 112 and 113.
Instead of the lentils, or as well as, you could serve Pomme Fondant, Confit of Garlic or Braised Cabbage (see pages 208, 207 and 209).

4 PORTIONS

4 woodcock
4 sprigs thyme
12 juniper berries
salt and freshly ground white pepper
8 slices streaky bacon
100 ml (3½ fl oz) goose fat

ROAST WOODCOCK ON TOAST *WITH RED WINE SAUCE*

TO SERVE

4 slices Brioche (SEE PAGE 217)
25 g (1 oz) unsalted butter
1 recipe Red Wine Sauce (SEE PAGE 195)

1. Preheat the oven to 200°C/400°F/Gas 6.
2. Place 1 sprig of thyme, 3 juniper berries, and salt and pepper inside each woodcock, then cover the breasts with the bacon. Tie them up for roasting, then season on the outside.
3. Heat the goose fat in a pan and seal the woodcock on all sides. Place into the preheated oven and roast for about 10-15 minutes, depending on size, making sure they are not overcooked. Allow to rest for 5 minutes when removed from the oven.
4. Fry the brioche slices gently in the butter, and allow to go nice and crisp as for fried bread.
5. Heat the sauce gently.
6. To serve, remove the breasts and legs from the woodcock, and place on top of the hot slice of brioche. Pour the sauce around.

CHEF'S NOTE
Suitable garnishes for roast woodcock are Confit of Garlic and/or Shallots, bacon, Braised Cabbage, Brussels sprouts, Wild Mushrooms and Pomme Fondant (see pages 207, 209, 137 and 208).

CHOUCROÛTE OF PARTRIDGE, *Jus Rôti*

4 PORTIONS

4 partridges
4 sprigs fresh thyme
12 juniper berries
8 slices streaky bacon
salt and freshly ground white pepper
100 ml (3½ fl oz) goose fat

CHOUCROÛTE

450 g (1 lb) choucroûte in Riesling
2 carrots, trimmed
50 g (2 oz) back bacon, cut into lardons
1 continental garlic sausage (SEE PAGE 85)
50 ml (2 fl oz) white wine
600 ml (1 pint) Chicken Stock (SEE PAGE 190)
1 bay leaf
2 sprigs thyme
10 juniper berries

TO SERVE

½ recipe Jus Rôti (SEE PAGE 195)

1. Put the choucroûte into a pan with the carrots, bacon, sausage and white wine, and simmer to reduce until virtually evaporated. Add the chicken stock, bay leaf, thyme and juniper berries, bring to the boil, season with salt and pepper and simmer very gently on top of the stove (or in the oven at 140-150°C/275-300°F/Gas 1-2) until the choucroûte becomes tender. This should take approximately 40 minutes, but remove the sausage after 25 minutes as this will be cooked. Slice the sausage, and put back into the choucroûte once it too is cooked.
2. Preheat the oven to 200°C/400°F/Gas 6.
3. Put into each partridge, at the parson's nose end, 1 sprig of thyme and 3 juniper berries. Season them inside at the neck end. Place 2 slices of bacon on the breasts, then tie them and season on the outside.
4. In a suitable roasting pan or tray, seal the partridges well in the goose fat on all sides, before placing in the preheated oven to roast, making sure you turn them at least two or three times for even cooking. They should take between 10 and 15 minutes, depending on size.
5. Remove the birds from the cooking pan and rest for 5-10 minutes. Do not throw away the fat or the juices from the birds.

6. Heat the sauce through gently. Do not boil it. Add the juices from the cooking pan (keep the fat for another use; it will have acquired flavour from the partridges), as well as the juices exuded by the resting birds.

7. To serve, place the choucroûte in the centre of the plate. Carefully remove the legs and breasts from the partridge carcasses, and arrange these on top of the choucroûte, then pour the sauce over and around. Although this is a complete dish, with a little bit of everything – the bird, sausage, carrot and cabbage – a nice accompaniment would be some boiled new potatoes.

CHEF'S NOTE

Choucroûte goes well with white game birds – with quail, and pheasant as well as partridge – because it is quite delicate, complementing rather than overpowering the flavour of the birds. It makes for a good balance.

117

ROAST GROUSE
PROPERLY GARNISHED

4 PORTIONS

4 grouse
8 slices streaky bacon
4 sprigs thyme
12 juniper berries
salt and freshly ground white pepper
100 ml (3½ fl oz) goose fat
4 slices back bacon

BREAD SAUCE

400 ml (14 fl oz) milk
1 slice onion
1 clove
4 slices bread, diced without crusts

GAME CRISPS

2 potatoes (Maris Piper)
vegetable oil for deep-frying

GRAVY

1 celery stalk, chopped
1 onion, peeled and chopped
1 carrot, peeled and chopped
2 garlic cloves, peeled and halved
100 ml (3½ fl oz) white wine (brandy is good too)
2 sprigs thyme
200 ml (7 fl oz) Veal Stock (SEE PAGE 192)

1.   Preheat the oven to 200°C/400°F/Gas 6.
2.   Arrange 2 pieces of streaky bacon across the breasts of each grouse, and into each bird put a sprig of thyme and 3 juniper berries. Season inside and out, then tie and truss, making sure the bacon is kept in place.
3.   For the bread sauce, boil the milk with the onion and clove. Once brought to the boil, remove the clove and remove from the heat. Cover the pan with cling film, and leave the milk and onion to infuse together for 10 minutes.
4.   Put the diced bread into a pan and add half the strained, infused milk. Break down with a fork, then season with salt and pepper. You are looking for a thin mashed potato consistency, so more milk can be added as required. Keep to one side.

ROAST GROUSE
PROPERLY GARNISHED

5. For the game crisps, peel and slice the potatoes very finely as for crisps, and place under running water for half an hour to remove the starch. When ready to cook, drain and dry very well. Deep-fry in hot oil until golden. Drain on absorbent paper to remove all excess oil, then season with salt. Keep warm.

6. To roast the grouse, heat the goose fat in a roasting pan and seal the grouse on all sides before placing in the preheated oven. This will take about 15-20 minutes, depending on the size of the birds. Rest for 5-10 minutes to allow the birds to relax, then remove the strings. Keep warm.

7. Meanwhile, grill or pan-fry the back bacon, and warm through the bread sauce.

8. Place the celery, onion, carrot and garlic into the pan in which the grouse cooked, and roast them on top of the stove to a nice golden colour. Add the white wine, the thyme, and a little salt and pepper, and boil until virtually evaporated. Add the veal stock and all the juices that have drained out of the birds. Bring to the boil and simmer for 3 minutes, then pass through a chinois sieve. (In the gravy you could also use the grouse necks, wing tips, livers, hearts and stomachs for flavour.)

9. To serve, arrange the grouse on the plate, with the bread sauce, game crisps and bacon on side dishes for people to help themselves.

CHEF'S NOTE

*B*russels sprouts are one of the best accompaniments for a traditional roast grouse. Trim, blanch and refresh beforehand, then reheat when needed in an emulsion of butter and water.

The game crisps can be deep-fried up to 20 minutes in advance. The longer they are left, the crisper they get.

119

4 PORTIONS

4 x 225 g (8 oz) wood pigeons
salt and freshly ground white pepper
50 ml (2 fl oz) goose fat

TO SERVE

1 recipe Pomme Fondant (SEE PAGE 208)
1 recipe Braised Cabbage (SEE PAGE 209)
1 recipe Jus of Thyme (SEE PAGE 197)
25 g (1 oz) unsalted butter
8 slices ventreche ham (or very finely sliced streaky
bacon)
12 cloves Confit of Garlic (SEE PAGE 207)
8 tiny sprigs thyme

**ROAST WOOD
PIGEON,**
*BRAISED
CABBAGE,
JUS OF THYME*

1.   Preheat the oven to 200°C/400°F/Gas 6.
2.   Season the pigeon and seal on both sides in a little of the goose fat. Place in the preheated oven and cook for 12 minutes only. Allow to rest for 4-5 minutes.
3.   Meanwhile, heat through the potato, the cabbage and the sauce. Add the butter in little pieces to the sauce, and allow to melt and blend in.
4.   Cook the ham or bacon lightly under a hot grill without colouring it. Fry the garlic in a dry pan to crisp it up.
5.   To serve, remove the breasts from each bird. Place the potato in the centre top of the plate with the cabbage below. Place the pigeon breasts on the cabbage, with the ham or bacon and sprigs of thyme on top. Pour the sauce around.

ROAST WOOD PIGEON, PERFUME OF CEPS, WHITE TRUFFLE OIL

4 PORTIONS

4 x 225 g (8 oz) wood pigeons
salt and freshly ground white pepper
vegetable oil

PERFUME OF CEPS

2 pigeon carcasses
100 g (4 oz) chicken wings
1 carrot, diced
celeriac skin, thoroughly washed and diced (SEE BELOW)
1 onion, peeled and diced
1.2 litres (2 pints) Chicken Stock (SEE PAGE 190)
1 bay leaf
1 sprig thyme
2 egg whites
25 g (1 oz) dried ceps

TO SERVE

2 carrots
1 small celeriac, peeled (use washed skin in the perfume of ceps, SEE ABOVE)
50 g (2 oz) fresh green beans
2 baby leeks
25 ml (1 fl oz) truffle oil

1. Remove the legs, wings, wishbones and undercarriages from the pigeons. You are left with a double breast on the ribcage.

2. To make the perfume of ceps – a consommé – chop the chicken wings, pigeon carcasses and trimmings, and in a thick-bottomed pan in a little vegetable oil, sauté them until golden brown. Add the diced vegetables and colour these as well. Add the chicken stock and herbs, and bring to the boil. Skim and lightly season, then simmer for 20 minutes, skimming regularly and allowing to reduce slightly. Pass the liquid through a muslin cloth and leave to cool.

3. Blitz the egg whites and dried ceps in a blender until the egg is frothy and the ceps are ground down. Place into a thick-bottomed pan with a little ice and slowly whisk in the cold stock. Place on to the stove, bring to the boil and gently whisk regularly. As it comes to the boil, whisk it well and allow to settle and form a crust. Do not boil from this point on, but simmer gently.

4.   Season lightly with salt and pepper and allow the stock to reduce to approximately 600 ml (1 pint). Pass through a muslin cloth. It should be perfectly clear and intensely flavoured.

5.   Meanwhile, preheat the oven to 200°C/400°F/Gas 6.

6.   Season the wood pigeons and pan-fry in a little oil to colour nicely on both breasts, then place in the preheated oven and roast for about 12 minutes. Remove the pigeons from the oven and rest for 4-5 minutes.

7.   Meanwhile prepare the garnish vegetables. Cut the carrots and celeriac into batons, and top and tail the green beans. Remove the root from the baby leeks, and cut down to about 5 cm (2 in) in length. Blanch the vegetables in boiling salted water and refresh in cold water.

8.   To serve, heat the perfume of ceps up, then add the garnish vegetables. Spoon into a soup plate, spreading the stock and vegetables evenly. Remove the pigeon breasts from the bone and place on top of the vegetables. Drip a little truffle oil over the meat and stock.

CHEF'S NOTE

Kitchen legend has it that a foolproof way of testing for complete clarity of a consommé such as the one above is to pick some up in a solid silver spoon. Any impurities will immediately be seen.

4 PORTIONS

4 x 225 g (8 oz) rabbit legs
salt and freshly ground white pepper
100 g (4 oz) crépinette (pig's caul fat), in 4 equal pieces
50 g (2 oz) unsalted butter

STUFFING

100 g (4 oz) calf's sweetbreads
100 g (4 oz) boiled ham, cut in 5 mm (¼ in) thick slices
50 g (2 oz) Chicken Mousse (SEE PAGE 214)

TO SERVE

225 g (8 oz) Fresh Pasta (SEE PAGE 215), cut into noodles
75 g (3 oz) unsalted butter   2 sprigs rosemary
1 recipe Double Chicken Butter (SEE PAGE 203)
20 small asparagus tips
20 baby leeks, about 5 cm (2 in) long

ROAST BALLOTINE OF RABBIT,
FRESH NOODLES, ROSEMARY BUTTER

1.   Bone the rabbit legs, so that only the small first bone is left. Cut the thigh cleanly. Season the insides of the legs with salt and pepper.
2.   To make the stuffing, bring the sweetbreads to the boil in a little salted water, then press flat between two plates. Remove all the membranes and cut into 5 mm (¼ in) dice.
3.   Cut the ham into 5 mm (¼ in) dice as well.
4.   Mix the sweetbread and ham dice with the chicken mousse, and stuff it into the rabbit legs. Roll around to make the shape again, then wrap each firmly in a piece of *crépinette*. Roll to a nice sausage shape with the little bone sticking out at one end. Wrap each very tightly in foil to a thin sausage shape, rather like a pig's trotter.
5.   Poach the stuffed rabbit legs for 12 minutes in simmering salted water, then allow to rest for 5 minutes.
6.   Meanwhile, reheat the noodles in 50 ml (2 fl oz) water with 50 g (2 oz) of the unsalted butter and 1 rosemary sprig.
7.   Melt the double chicken butter, and leave the remaining rosemary sprig in it to infuse for 10 minutes. Pass through a chinois sieve just before serving and heat again.
8.   Separately, blanch, refresh and reheat the asparagus and leeks in an emulsion of the remaining unsalted butter and a couple of tablespoons of water.
9.   Remove the rabbit legs from the foil, and fry gently to brown all over in the butter. Slice into three - two good slices and the piece with the bone - and arrange in the centre of the plates. Place the noodles at the top, the vegetables at the side, and the double chicken butter sauce beside the meat.

8 PORTIONS

1 x 6.3 kg (14 lb) suckling pig, without the head
vegetable oil
salt and freshly ground white pepper

APPLE SAUCE

6 Granny Smith apples
50 g (2 oz) unsalted butter
juice of ½ lemon   caster sugar

TO SERVE

32 each of baby carrots, baby leeks and
small asparagus stalks
24 baby fennel bulbs
32 small new potatoes, skinned and turned
100 g (4 oz) unsalted butter
50 g (2 oz) small marjoram leaves
1 recipe Jus Rôti (SEE PAGE 195)
24 sprigs chervil

ROAST SUCKLING PIG

1. Have the butcher bone the pig out, and roll it so that it looks like a whole loin, with skin and crackling all round. Tie neatly, and score lightly.

2. Preheat the oven to 180°C/350°F/Gas 4.

3. Brush the crackling with a little vegetable oil and sprinkle with a little salt. Roast in the preheated oven for 1½ hours, turning every 15 minutes.

4. Meanwhile blanch the baby vegetables separately in boiling salted water until *croquant* (slightly crunchy), then refresh in iced water. Cook the potatoes in boiling water until thoroughly cooked.

5. For the apple sauce, peel and core the apples, and cut them into small pieces. Sweat in the butter with the lemon juice and a pinch of sugar. Allow the apples to break down to a purée.

6. When the joint is cooked, remove from the oven, and remove the crackling from the meat. Put the crackling back into a hotter oven to crisp if required. Keep the meat warm.

7. To reheat the baby vegetables and potatoes, pass through an emulsion of the butter and a little water. Season with salt as required.

8. Put the marjoram into the sauce and heat gently.

9. To serve, slice the joint into nice slices, and arrange on the plate. Arrange the baby vegetables and the potatoes neatly over the meat, with some crackling on top. Pour the sauce over the meat, and decorate with chervil. Serve the apple sauce on the side.

ROAST HAM

WITH A
BITTERSWEET PORT
WINE SAUCE

UP TO 12 PORTIONS

1 x 1.5-1.8 kg (3½-4 lb) ham
12 cloves
200 ml (7 fl oz) vegetable oil
225 g (8 oz) liquid honey

TO SERVE

3 x recipes Bittersweet Port Wine Sauce (SEE PAGE 197)

1. Leave the ham under running cold water for 2 days to remove as much salt as possible. Or soak in water to cover, changing the water every so often.
2. Bring the ham to the boil in fresh cold water to cover, and simmer for 1-1½ hours.
3. Preheat the oven to 180°C/350°F/Gas 4.
4. Remove the ham from the water and the pan, and cut off the skin. Score the fat evenly into neat 1 cm (½ in) squares or diamonds, and stud all over with the cloves.
5. Pour over the vegetable oil and place in the preheated oven for 2 hours. Brush well with the honey every 5 or so minutes. If the fat fails to crisp, turn the oven up to 220°C/425°F/Gas 7 at the end, about 5 minutes.
6. To serve, warm up the sauce and chosen accompanying vegetables. Carve the ham into nice thick slices, and serve warm with the sauce.

CHEF'S NOTE

This is a good dish for a dinner party. Any type of potato dish would be a good accompaniment, as would Braised Cabbage (see page 209).

Start preparing this dish 2 days in advance.

4 PORTIONS

1 best end of lamb
zest of ½ orange and ½ lemon
10 g (¼ oz) each of flat parsley, rosemary and thyme leaves
1 garlic clove, peeled
salt
250 g (9 oz) crépinette (pig's caul fat), in one piece

TO SERVE

1 recipe Pomme Fondant or Anna
(SEE PAGE 208)
1 recipe Lamb Sauce (SEE PAGE 191)
about 50 g (2 oz) unsalted butter
1 tomato, skinned, seeded and diced
2 sprigs flat parsley
1 small sprig each of thyme and rosemary

1. Remove the meat from the bones, making sure the fat is kept intact and in one piece. Remove the meat from the fat, and trim the meat. Place the fat between two sheets of cling film and bat out until very thin.

2. Chop the lemon and orange zest very finely until almost a purée. Do the same with the herbs. Using a little salt, grind the garlic to a paste.

3. Mix the herbs, garlic and zest together, then smear across the front of the meat, using a palette knife.

4. Place the meat back on to the fat and roll the fat around the meat. Wrap in the *crépinette,* and tie with string. Place in the fridge and allow to rest for 2 days.

5. Preheat the oven to 220°C/425°F/Gas 7.

6. Roast the lamb in the preheated oven for about 10 minutes. Remove from the oven and leave to rest for about 5 minutes.

7. Heat through the potatoes and the sauce. Add half the butter, the diced tomato and the parsley leaves to the sauce at the last moment.

8. To serve, bring the remaining butter to a froth, then add the thyme and rosemary. Baste the lamb gently with this, then slice and serve immediately with the potato and sauce.

ROAST SADDLE OF LAMB
WITH JUNIPER JUS

1 x 2.25 kg (5 lb) saddle of lamb, boned
salt and freshly ground white pepper
Dijon mustard
450 g (1 lb) crépinette (pig's caul fat), in one large piece
100 ml (3½ fl oz) vegetable oil

STUFFING

6 lamb's kidneys
2 shallots, peeled and finely diced
50 g (2 oz) unsalted butter
100 ml (3½ fl oz) port
600 g (1¼ lb) fresh spinach   1 egg

TO SERVE

2 recipes Juniper Jus (SEE PAGE 196)
25 g (1 oz) hard unsalted butter, diced
2 recipes Pomme Fondant (SEE PAGE 208)
18-24 cloves Confit of Garlic (SEE PAGE 207)
fleur de sel   thyme sprigs

1.   Preheat the oven to 200°C/400°F/Gas 6.
2.   To prepare the stuffing, skin and remove all the veins from the kidneys. Cut in half, discard all the fat, and cut the kidneys into small dice.
3.   Sweat the shallot in the butter until golden brown. Throw in the kidney dice and allow to colour nicely, then add the port and reduce until almost evaporated. Leave to cool.
4.   Wash the spinach, remove any tough stalks, then cook in boiling salted water. Refresh in cold water, then squeeze dry and chop roughly. Leave to cool.
5.   Mix the kidneys and spinach together with the egg and plenty of salt and pepper.
6.   Trim any excess fat off the saddle and place on the work surface, skin side down. Trim the flaps and season the meat. Spread it with a little Dijon mustard all over. Put the stuffing inside, fold over the two fillets and flaps on top, and roll up. Wrap in the *crépinette* at least three times, then tie nicely.
7.   Seal the rolled saddle all over in a little oil, then roast in the preheated oven for 30-40 minutes. When cooked, allow to rest for 15 minutes.
8.   Heat the sauce through gently, adding the butter dice at the last moment. Heat the potatoes. Fry the garlic in a dry pan to crisp it up.
9.   To serve, place a pomme fondant and 3 garlic cloves at the top of the plate. Slice one thick slice of lamb and place below the fondant with the sauce poured around. Sprinkle a little *fleur de sel* on the meat, and garnish with thyme.

ROAST RUMP OF LAMB
WITH VEGETABLES, SAUCE PALOISE

4 PORTIONS

4 x 225 g (8 oz) rumps of lamb
salt and freshly ground white pepper
100 ml (3½ fl oz) vegetable oil
25 g (1 oz) unsalted butter

TO SERVE

8 baby fennel bulbs, trimmed
12 baby leeks, trimmed
12 fine asparagus tips
12 baby carrots, trimmed
50 g (2 oz) unsalted butter
caster sugar
12 cloves Confit of Garlic (SEE PAGE 207)
1 recipe Lamb Sauce (SEE PAGE 191)
1 recipe Sauce Paloise (SEE PAGE 202)
thyme sprigs

1.   Preheat the oven to 220°C/425°F/Gas 7.
2.   Season the rumps of lamb, then pan-fry in the oil, adding the butter during the cooking. Cook in the preheated oven until medium rare, approximately 15 minutes. Remove from the oven and the pan and allow to rest for about 5-10 minutes.
3.   Meanwhile, cook the fennel, leeks and asparagus separately in boiling salted water until still crisp, then refresh in iced water.
4.   Cook the baby carrots in 25 g (1 oz) of the butter, with a pinch each of salt and sugar, and a little water. Allow an emulsion to form around the carrots.
5.   Pan-fry the cloves of garlic in a dry pan so they become crisp.
6.   Reheat the green vegetables in boiling water, then pass through an emulsion of the remaining butter and a little hot water.
7.   Heat the lamb sauce through gently. Add the mint leaves to the sauce paloise at the very last minute.
8.   To serve, cut the lamb into thin slices, approximately 10 per rump, and arrange on the plate in a semi-circle. Arrange the vegetables haphazardly over the lamb. Pour the lamb sauce around, and serve the sauce paloise separately. Garnish with thyme.

ROAST SADDLE OF LAMB FORESTIÈRE

6-8 PORTIONS

1 x 2.25 kg (5 lb) saddle of lamb, boned
Dijon mustard
salt and freshly ground white pepper
450 g (1 lb) crépinette (pig's caul fat), in one
large piece
100 ml (3½ fl oz) vegetable oil

STUFFING

14 garlic cloves, peeled
6 small shallots, peeled
120 ml (4 fl oz) goose fat
100 g (4 oz) ventreche ham (or very finely sliced
streaky bacon), diced
200 g (7 oz) celeriac, peeled and diced
200 g (7 oz) button mushrooms, sliced
100 g (4 oz) trompettes de mort mushrooms, prepared
100 g (4 oz) girolles, prepared
400 g (14 oz) spinach
1 egg

TO SERVE

2 x recipes Lamb Sauce (SEE PAGE 191)
2 recipes Pomme Fondant (SEE PAGE 208)
12-24 cloves Confit of Garlic (SEE PAGE 207)

1.   Trim any excess fat off the saddle, and place on the work surface, skin side down. Trim the flaps, rub Dijon mustard on to the meaty inside, and season with salt and pepper.
2.   To prepare the stuffing, cook the garlic and shallots in the goose fat gently for about 20 minutes or until soft. When soft, remove and drain well. Add the diced ventreche ham and celeriac to the goose fat, and cook until soft without colouring. Remove and drain well. Add the three types of mushrooms to the goose fat, and sweat until soft. Remove and drain well. Mix all the 'confit' ingredients together, and allow to cool.
3.   Wash the spinach three times in cold water. Blanch in boiling salted water, then refresh and squeeze dry. Chop finely, and leave to cool.
4.   Preheat the oven to 200°C/400°F/Gas 6.

5. Mix the spinach with all the confit ingredients - the mushrooms, ham, celeriac, shallot and garlic. Mix in the beaten egg and salt and pepper to taste. Place down the centre of the saddle of lamb, just covering the two loins. Fold over the fillets and the flaps, and wrap in the *crépinette,* at least three times. Tie with string.

6. Seal the lamb all over in the hot oil in a pan, then place in the preheated oven for 30-40 minutes. When cooked, allow to rest for 15 minutes.

7. Heat the potatoes and sauce. Pan-fry the garlic confit in a dry pan to make it crisp.

8. To serve, place a pomme fondant and 2-3 garlic cloves at the top of the plate. Slice one thick slice of lamb and place below the fondant, with the sauce poured around.

STEAK BÉARNAISE

4 PORTIONS

4 x 225 g (8 oz) sirloin steaks, trimmed
salt and freshly ground white pepper
vegetable oil if necessary

TO SERVE

1 recipe Béarnaise Sauce (SEE PAGE 202)

1. Season and cook the sirloins in a red-hot, ridged cast-iron pan or under a red-hot grill until medium rare, about 3-4 minutes on each side, depending on thickness.
2. Add the tarragon to the sauce at the last minute, when the steak is cooked.
3. To serve, place the steak on a hot plate, with the sauce.

CHEF'S NOTE

Suitable garnishes for this dish are chips, Pomme Fondant, Pomme Anna (see page 208), grilled tomato, grilled mushrooms or mixed salad.

4 PORTIONS

4 x 175 g (6 oz) fillet steaks, trimmed
salt and freshly ground white pepper
100 ml (3½ fl oz) vegetable oil

WILD MUSHROOMS

100 g (4 oz) mixed wild mushrooms (preferably morels,
girolles, ceps and trompettes de mort) according to
season
75 g (3 oz) unsalted butter
1 shallot, peeled and finely chopped
1 tomato, skinned, seeded and diced
1 teaspoon snipped chives

TO SERVE

1 recipe Pomme Rösti (SEE PAGE 209)
1 recipe Madeira Sauce (SEE PAGE 194)

FILLET OF BEEF FORESTIÈRE, POMME RÖSTI, MADEIRA SAUCE

1.   Make the pomme rösti and the sauce, and keep warm.
2.   Wash and prepare the mushrooms, then separately sauté each in 15 g (½ oz) of the butter. (This can be done about 1 hour in advance.)
3.   When ready to finally cook and serve, season the steaks and pan-fry in the oil until cooked to your liking – preferably medium rare, about 3-4 minutes on each side, but depending on thickness. You could fry it for a shorter time, then flash into a well preheated hot oven, at 250°C/500°F/the highest gas, for a minute or two.
4.   Reheat the mushrooms by sautéing them in the remaining butter with the shallot. Add the diced tomato, chives and seasoning at the last moment.
5.   To serve, place a pomme rösti on each plate, with a steak on top. Arrange the mushrooms around the steak, and pour the sauce over.

CHEF'S NOTE

This dish is expensive, using four fillet steaks, but we like to offer it occasionally at the Canteen — it's one of our 'specials'.

To ensure a good shape to your steaks, buy the fillet in one piece. Wrap it in cling film, roll out evenly, and chill to 'set' for 24 hours. Cut into steaks, then pan-fry with the cling film still in place around the outside diameter. Remove the cling film before serving.

ROAST RUMP STEAK BORDELAISE

*S*tart this recipe the day before.

4 PORTIONS

4 x 175 g (6 oz) rump steaks, well hung
100 ml (3½ fl oz) vegetable oil
25 g (1 oz) unsalted butter
24 pieces marrow bone, 5 mm (¼ in) thick
salt and coarsely crushed white peppercorns

TO SERVE

4 shallots, peeled and finely chopped
100 ml (3½ fl oz) each of red wine and port
1 recipe Red Wine Sauce (SEE PAGE 195)

1.   Marinate the shallot in a mixture of the wine and port for 24 hours.
2.   Simmer the shallot mixture to reduce down until it has almost evaporated. Add to the sauce and warm through gently.
3.   Pan-fry the steaks in the hot oil for 3 minutes on each side, depending on thickness. Add the butter half-way through the cooking.
4.   When the steaks are cooked, remove from the pan and allow to rest for 5 minutes.
5   Meanwhile, have ready a small pan of simmering salted water in which to cook the pieces of marrow bone. Cook for about 2 minutes. Drain well, and remove the marrow from the bones just as serving the steaks.
6.   To serve, place the steak on the plate and pour the sauce over and around it. Place the marrow pieces on top of each steak, and season it with a little salt and coarsely crushed white (*mignonette*) pepper.

BRAISED OXTAIL IN CRÉPINETTE, *FUMET OF RED WINE*

This dish needs to be started a day or so in advance.

4 PORTIONS

2.25 kg (5 lb) oxtail, trimmed and jointed
750 ml (1¼ pints) red wine   vegetable oil
salt and freshly ground white pepper
3 large carrots, washed   2 large onions
3 celery stalks, washed   1 whole head of garlic
5 ml (2 fl oz) cooking brandy
30 g (1¼ oz) plain flour
2.5 litres (4¼ pints) Veal Stock (SEE PAGE 192)
1 sprig thyme   1 bay leaf   1 small celeriac
200 g (7 oz) crépinette (pig's caul fat)

SAUCE

500 ml (17 fl oz) red wine   150 ml (5 fl oz) port
25 g (1 oz) hard unsalted butter, diced
1 teaspoon double cream

1. Trim any excess fat from the outside of the pieces of oxtail, then marinate in the red wine overnight.
2. Drain well, and pat the oxtail dry on a cloth. Pass the red wine through a fine sieve, place in a pan on the stove and boil to reduce by three-quarters.
3. Coat the base of a large, thick-bottomed pan with vegetable oil and heat until almost smoking. Season the oxtail pieces with salt and pepper and seal them all over in the hot oil until they are a good, deep, dark colour. Drain.
4. Peel two of the carrots and both the onions, and cut them and the celery into large pieces. Cut the garlic head in half.
5. Gently fry the chopped vegetables and garlic in the same oil in the pan until they are golden brown.
6. Add the brandy to this and cook until it has almost evaporated.
7. Add the reduced red wine marinade, skimmed of any impurities, and continue to reduce.
8. When almost a syrup, add the sealed oxtail pieces and stir into the syrupy wine.
9. Sprinkle in the flour (browned in a dry pan for extra flavour if you like), and stir together. Continue to cook for 5 minutes.
10. Pour in 2 litres (3½ pints) of the veal stock, bring to the boil and turn down to a gentle simmer. Add the thyme and bay leaf, cover with a lid and cook gently either on top of the stove or in the oven preheated to 160°C/325°F/Gas 3, for approximately 2½-3 hours or until tender enough for the meat to come easily off the bones.

11. Drain the oxtail from the cooking liquid and remove and discard all the pieces of vegetable.

12. Pass the cooking liquid through a fine strainer and then through muslin cloth about three or four times to remove all the impurities and solids.

13. Take one-third of the cooking liquid and reduce it on the stove until very thick. Remove and keep warm. The other two-thirds will be used to make the sauce (see below).

14. Remove all the meat carefully from the oxtails, keeping it in fairly large pieces rather than flakes. Leave behind as much fat and gristle as possible.

15. Peel the celeriac and the remaining carrot and cut them into 1.5 cm (¾ in) dice. Cook these separately in a little of the hot vegetable oil until golden brown. Drain and cool.

16. Add the above vegetable dice and the reduced third of the cooking liquid to the pieces of oxtail. Gently combine and allow to cool.

17. When cool, mould the mixture into four portion-size balls. A 120 ml (4 fl oz) ladle is good for this. Then wrap the balls individually in cling film and allow to 'set' in the fridge.

18. When using caul fat, make sure it is well washed and that all the blood is removed. (The best way to do this is to sit it under cold running water for about 8 hours.)

19. Cut the caul fat into four pieces without holes or large veins of fat. Lay one piece flat on the work surface. Unwrap one oxtail 'ball' from its cling film and place on the caul fat. Roll the caul fat around the ball and fix the two ends of the caul fat together under the ball. Do the same with the remaining balls.

20. To make the sauce, reduce the red wine and port together until a syrup, and then add the remaining two-thirds of the cooking liquor. Reduce this until of a consistency that will coat the back of a spoon.

21. Whisk the hard butter into the sauce to enrich it and give it a glossy shine, then add the cream. This helps stabilise the sauce. Keep to one side.

22. To reheat the oxtail balls, place them in the remaining veal stock in a small saucepan – the stock should cover them by one-third – and put in the oven preheated to 220°C/425°F/Gas 7 for a minimum of 10 minutes. Coat them continually with the stock so that they have a glaze.

23. Reheat the sauce and correct the seasoning.

24. Serve an oxtail ball on a puddle of the sauce, with a little on top as well.

4 x 150 g (5 oz) slices calf's liver, 5 mm-1 cm (¼-½ in)
thick
salt and freshly ground white pepper
plain flour
vegetable oil

TO SERVE

1 recipe Braised Lettuce (SEE PAGE 210)
½ recipe Sauce Diable (SEE PAGE 196)
12 sage leaves
8 slices ventreche ham (or very finely sliced streaky
bacon)

ESCALOPE OF CALF'S LIVER, VENTRECHE HAM, BRAISED LETTUCE, SAUCE DIABLE

1. Make or briefly heat through the braised lettuce.
2. Warm through the sauce gently.
3. Deep-fry the sage leaves in hot vegetable oil, then drain well on absorbent kitchen paper. Season with a little salt.
4. Lightly grill the ham or bacon without colouring.
5. Season and flour the liver, dusting off any excess. Pan-fry in 100 ml (3½ fl oz) hot oil until pink, a minute or so on each side, depending on thickness.
6. To serve, place the braised lettuce on the plate, with the liver on top and the sauce over and around. Place the bacon and sage on top of the liver.

CHEF'S NOTE
I've eaten calf's liver in any number of ways, but I still think that it's best served with bacon and a good sauce.

ESCALOPE OF CALF'S LIVER
WITH LIME, BRAISED LETTUCE AND POMME SABLÉ

4 PORTIONS

4 x 150 g (5 oz) slices calf's liver, 5 mm-1 cm (¼-½ in)
thick
salt and freshly ground white pepper
plain flour
100 ml (3½ fl oz) vegetable oil

TO SERVE

2 limes
1 recipe Braised Lettuce (SEE PAGE 210)
1 recipe Pomme Sablé (SEE PAGE 207)
½ recipe Lime Jus (SEE PAGE 198)

1.   Cut the zest off the limes, and confit it as on page 221. Keep the denuded limes.
2.   Make or briefly heat through the braised lettuce.
3.   Prepare or heat through the pomme sablé.
4.   Segment the limes from which the zest was cut; use the segments as garnish. Squeeze the juice from what is left of the limes into the sauce.
5.   Season and flour the liver, dusting off any excess. Pan-fry in the hot oil until pink, a minute or so on each side, depending on thickness.
6.   Reheat the sauce very gently, mixing in the lime juice.
7.   To serve, place the pomme sablé at the top of the plate. Place some braised lettuce below the potato. Put the calf's liver on top of the lettuce, and the sauce over the liver. Sprinkle lime zest and lime segments over the liver.

CHEF'S NOTE

Many people like liver to be very thin, but the thinner it is, the less control you have over the cooking. The ideal thickness is 5 mm-1 cm (¼-½ in).

PUDDINGS

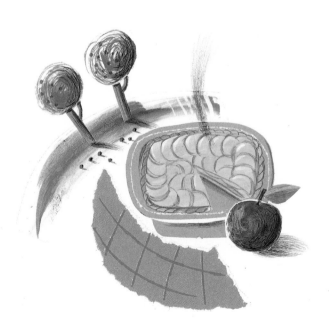

PUDDINGS

FOR MANY RESTAURANT CUSTOMERS, the puddings are what they really look forward to. Often, though, I'm afraid they can be really disappointed – a tart may have been made the day before and have lost its sparkle, a mousse may have been sitting too long and is too cool and rubbery. At The Canteen we make the puddings for lunchtime in the morning, and then make a second lot for the evening rush. Some puddings, of course, need to be made a little in advance, like the baked terrine dishes, or the frozen parfaits, but even ice creams and sorbets we like to serve as fresh as possible.

The majority of our puddings are fruit based in some form or other. We combine fruit with eggs in a soufflé, with and in ice cream or sorbet, with and in a mousse, in a jelly, in fruit tarts, with pastry and meringue. We even bake an apple stuffed with our own mincemeat.

We also use chocolate a lot, both white and dark, primarily because people want it and expect it. The tarts we offer, both hot and cold, are often served with ice cream, a happy combination in terms of flavour and texture – the crisp pastry contrasting with the creaminess of the ice or sorbet. We also serve a number of popular classics, such as crème brûlée, which sings of vanilla, and bread and butter pudding.

Sometimes the little extras are what make a pudding more special and spectacular – the tulip baskets look wonderful encasing a simple scoop of ice cream; the sugar cage adds glamour; and a few shreds of confit of citrus zest add texture and flavour. Even a simple raspberry sauce, a purée of fruit and sugar, gives colour and flavour, and brings the *look* of the plate together.

RED WINE JELLY

4 PORTIONS

250 g (9 oz) caster sugar
325 ml (11 fl oz) red wine
2 star anise
4 gelatine leaves, soaked in cold water to soften
1 punnet raspberries
1 punnet strawberries
1 punnet blackberries
1 punnet blueberries

TO SERVE

1 recipe Raspberry (or other red fruit) Coulis
(SEE PAGE 220)

1.   To make up the jelly, put the sugar and red wine into a suitable pan with the star anise, and melt the sugar over a gentle heat. Take off the heat, add the softened gelatine, and leave to cool but not set.
2.   Arrange a layer of raspberries on the bottom of 4 dariole moulds. Pour over a little jelly and leave it to set, then add a layer of thinly sliced strawberries, more jelly, a layer of blackberries and blueberries mixed, more jelly and repeat with strawberries and jelly as a final layer. Leave to set each time between layers. Refrigerate for 30-60 minutes.
3.   To serve, turn the jelly out on to a plate (dip the base of the moulds briefly in hot water). Accompany with the fruit coulis and some extra red fruit if you like.

CHEF'S NOTE
Everyone makes summer pudding during the soft fruit season, but this is a much better alternative — it's cleaner, lighter and much fresher.

CHAMPAGNE JELLY
WITH PASSIONFRUIT SAUCE

4 PORTIONS

1 mango
1 small Charentais melon
1 papaya   1 small punnet raspberries

CHAMPAGNE JELLY

325 ml (11 fl oz) champagne
300 g (11 oz) caster sugar
6 gelatine leaves, soaked in cold water to soften

TO SERVE

1 recipe Passionfruit Sauce (SEE PAGE 220)

1.   To make up the jelly, dissolve the sugar in the champagne over a gentle heat. Remove from the heat and add the softened gelatine. Leave to cool but not set.

2.   Peel the mango, then cut into it in two places to remove the flat stone. Remove all the flesh in as neat and small pieces as possible.

3.   Cut the melon in half and remove and discard the seeds. Remove the skin and cut the flesh into neat small pieces. Do the same with the papaya.

4.   Pour a little of the cold jelly into the bottom of each of 4 dariole moulds. Place the raspberries in this, point down, and leave to set. Arrange some pieces of papaya in next, cover with jelly and leave to set. Make similar layers with the melon and lastly the mango. Fill to the top with jelly, cover with cling film, and leave to set.

5.   To serve, turn out on to a serving plate (dip the base of the moulds briefly in hot water). Serve with the passionfruit sauce.

4 PORTIONS

4 egg whites
120 g (4½ oz) caster sugar
120 g (4½ oz) icing sugar

RASPBERRY SORBET

500 g (18 oz) raspberry purée
70 g (2¾ oz) caster sugar
70 ml (2¾ fl oz) glucose syrup

BERRY COMPOTE

100 g (4 oz) raspberries
50 g (2 oz) blackberries
50 g (2 oz) blackcurrants
50 g (2 oz) redcurrants
85 ml (3 fl oz) Raspberry Coulis (SEE PAGE 220)

TO SERVE

100 ml (3½ fl oz) double cream, whipped
a few fresh redcurrants

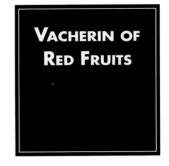

VACHERIN OF RED FRUITS

1. Preheat the oven to 100°C/220°F/a little less than Gas ¼.
2. To make the meringue, whip the egg whites until stiff, then add the caster sugar slowly, whipping continually, until thick and glossy. Finally fold in the icing sugar. Spoon into a piping bag and pipe the meringue into flat spiral discs about 5 cm (2 in) in diameter on a baking tray lined with silicone paper. You need at least 8 spirals. Cook in the preheated oven for 2 hours.
3. To make the sorbet, heat the raspberry purée with the sugar and glucose syrup until the sugar dissolves. Cool over ice and churn in an ice-cream machine until frozen, about 15-20 minutes, or freeze in the freezer.
4. To make the vacherins, pipe the raspberry sorbet in a layer between two meringue discs. Place in the freezer until ready to serve. Make at least 4.
5. To make the berry compote, cook the fruit in the coulis for 3-4 minutes until warm only, then leave to cool.
6. To serve, place a vacherin on each plate, and pour the berry compote around. Finish with a quenelle of double cream, topped with some fresh redcurrants.

FEUILLANTINE OF RED FRUITS

4 PORTIONS

200 g (7 oz) Puff Pastry (SEE PAGE 215)
icing sugar
450 g (1 lb) mixed berries (choose from raspberries,
wild strawberries, blueberries, redcurrants, blackberries)
1 recipe Raspberry Coulis (SEE PAGE 220)

SABAYON OF KIRSCH

1 egg   1 egg yolk
25 g (1 oz) caster sugar
1 gelatine leaf, melted in a little water
350 ml (12 fl oz) double cream
2 tablespoons Kirsch

TO SERVE

Confit of Citrus Zest (SEE PAGE 221)
mint sprigs

1.   Roll the pastry out on a work surface sprinkled with icing sugar to a rectangle about 3 mm (⅛ in) thick. Roll the rectangle up like a Swiss roll and chill for 2 hours.
2.   Slice the puff pastry roll into circles 1 cm (½ in) thick, and roll out each circle until paper thin. Place on non-stick paper on baking trays, and cut into tidy circles using a plain 10 cm (4 in) cutter. Rest for an hour in the fridge.
3.   Meanwhile preheat the oven to 220°C/425°F/Gas 7.
4.   Bake the circles in the preheated oven for about 15 minutes or until golden brown. As soon as you take them out of the oven, press flat immediately with the clean base of a heavy pan. You want the circles to be completely flat, not risen like conventional puff pastry. Leave to cool.
5.   To make the sabayon, mix the egg and egg yolk with the sugar in a bowl over a bain-marie, and whisk over gentle heat until warm, then cool down.
6.   Add the melted gelatine to the egg mixture and mix in well.
7.   Whip the double cream to firm peaks, whisk in the Kirsch, then mix with the egg mixture. Chill for 30 minutes.
8.   Keeping a few separate for garnish, mix all the berries in a bowl, together with about half of the coulis.
9.   To serve, spoon some coulis on to each plate. Place a puff pastry disc on top, and top that with 2 drained tablespoons of the mixed berries. Top this in turn with 1 tablespoon of the sabayon. Place another puff pastry disc on top, dust with icing sugar, and decorate with the orange zest, the mint and the retained berries.

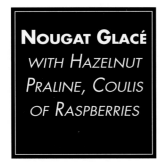

NOUGAT GLACÉ
WITH HAZELNUT PRALINE, COULIS OF RASPBERRIES

15 PORTIONS

150 g (5 oz) shelled hazelnuts
425 g (15 oz) caster sugar
6 egg whites
450 ml (15 fl oz) double cream

TO SERVE

3 recipes Raspberry Coulis (SEE PAGE 220)

1.   Preheat the oven to 230°C/450°F/Gas 8. Line a terrine 30 x 7.5 cm (12 x 3 in) with greaseproof paper. Set the freezer to its coldest.
2.   To start the praline base of the nougat, warm the hazelnuts in the preheated oven for about 3-4 minutes, or until golden brown. Skin quickly by rubbing in a cloth. Chop roughly.
3.   Heat 150 g (5 oz) of the sugar in a heavy-based pan to melt and make a caramel. Stir in the warm toasted hazelnuts, and pour on to a cold oiled tray. Leave to cool and set. When cold crush into small pieces, using a rolling pin.
4.   Whip the egg whites and the remaining sugar together to make a stiff meringue.
5.   Whip the cream to stiff peaks, then fold together gently with the meringue and crushed praline until mixed.
6.   Fill the terrine to the top with the mixture, and place in the freezer until hard, at least 24 hours.
7.   To serve, remove the terrine from the freezer, and from the dish. Cut into slices and serve either surrounded by the coulis or on top of the coulis.

CHEF'S NOTE

Make this frozen dessert a day in advance. You must turn the freezer to its very coldest setting beforehand, otherwise the caramel will start to dissolve.

14-16 PORTIONS

500 g (18 oz) Mascarpone cheese
50 g (18 oz) double cream
3 eggs
200 g (7 oz) caster sugar
1 recipe Chocolate Roulade (SEE PAGE 183)
200 ml (7 fl oz) Amaretto liqueur
100 ml (3½ fl oz) very strong sweet espresso coffee

ICED TIRAMISU PARFAIT,
COFFEE CRÈME ANGLAISE

TO SERVE

2 recipes Coffee Crème Anglaise (SEE PAGE 219)

1. Using a spoon, combine the Mascarpone and the cream.
2. Whisk the eggs until fluffy and to the ribbon stage - when the lifted beater leaves a ribbon trail on the surface.
3. Put the sugar and a tablespoon or so of water into a heavy-bottomed pan, and cook to the soft ball stage - when a drop of the syrup moulded into a ball in iced water loses its shape when taken out of the water. (Using a sugar thermometer, this is when it registers 113-118°C/235-245°F.)
4. Add the syrup to the egg mixture and continue to whisk until the mixture is cold.
5. Whisk in the Mascarpone mixture until it forms soft peaks.
6. Cut the chocolate roulade into 4 rectangles to fit a large terrine (30 x 11 x 10 cm/ 12 x 4½ x 4 in), fully lined with silicone paper. Moisten these rectangles briefly in a mixture of the Amaretto and espresso coffee.
7. Put the cheese mixture into a piping bag and pipe a layer (using about a quarter) into the base of the terrine. Put a moistened roulade rectangle on top, and then repeat these layers three times more, ending with roulade. Cover the top with foil, and freeze.
8. To serve, bring out of the freezer at least 5 minutes in advance of eating. Turn out of the terrine, and cut a thin slice. Place on the plate, and spoon the coffee crème anglaise around.

CHEF'S NOTE

This may seem complicated, but terrines are useful in that they can be made in advance and frozen. You could cut them in half and freeze half for your next party.

TIRAMISU

8 PORTIONS

1 egg
70 g (2¾ oz) caster sugar
125 g (4½ oz) Mascarpone cheese
120 ml (4 fl oz) double cream

TO FINISH AND SERVE

16 Biscuits Cuillères (SEE PAGE 217)
about 100 ml (3½ fl oz) espresso coffee
about 50 ml (2 fl oz) Amaretto
8 cooked and shaped Tuiles or Tulip Baskets
(SEE PAGE 217)
cocoa powder

1. To make the tiramisu cream, whisk the egg and sugar together in a bowl in a bain-marie until it reaches 50°C/122°F. Take out of the bain-marie, and cool the sabayon by whisking firmly.

2. Cream together the Mascarpone cheese and the double cream, and whisk into the cold sabayon until smooth. Set aside.

3. A few minutes before you want to serve, soak 8 of the biscuits cuillères in a mixture of the espresso coffee and Amaretto.

4. To assemble, place the tulip baskets on individual plates, and pour a little tiramisu cream over the bottom. Place a soaked biscuit cuillère on top, then top with more cream to the rim of the tulip case. Dust with cocoa powder and serve with the remaining biscuits to dip.

CHEF'S NOTE

You could make the tiramisu in a coffee cup or similar, instead of in the tulip basket. It's an easy pudding, especially when you haven't got much time. Use bought langue de chat biscuits if you like.

156

8-10 PORTIONS

200 g (7 oz) Crème Pâtissière (SEE PAGE 219)
400 g (14 oz) white chocolate, broken into pieces
600 ml (1 pint) double cream, semi-whipped

TO SERVE

150 g (5 oz) white chocolate
150 g (5 oz) good dark chocolate
Orange Confit (SEE PAGE 221)
1 recipe Grand Marnier Crème Anglaise (SEE PAGE 219)
Confit of Citrus Zest (SEE PAGE 221)
16-20 sprigs mint

WHITE CHOCOLATE MOUSSE

1.   Make the crème pâtissière and use while warm.
2.   Melt the white chocolate in a bowl over a bain-marie (don't let it get too hot), then add to the warm crème pâtissière. Leave to cool.
3.   Fold the whipped cream into the white chocolate mixture and spoon into a tray measuring about 25 x 14 cm (10 x 5½ in), and at least 2.5 cm (1 in) deep. Leave to set.
4.   When set, cut into neat diamonds (or circles or squares), trimming the edges if necessary. You need 8 to 10 diamonds, one per portion.
5.   To make little chocolate diamonds (or circles or squares) to garnish the mousse, in two separate bowls in a bain-marie, melt 50 g (2 oz) each of the white and dark chocolate. Don't allow them to get too hot.
6.   Chop the remaining dark chocolate finely and add it to the melted dark chocolate. Spread this roughly, using a palette knife, into a large, very flat tray, lightly greased and covered with cling film. Leave 'holes' where you will later spread the white chocolate. Leave to set.
7.   Do the same with the white chocolate, adding the finely chopped white chocolate to the melted white chocolate. Spread this over the dark chocolate, so that both colours can be seen. Smooth the top, and leave to set.
8.   Cut the chocolate sheet carefully, using a hot knife, into diamonds (or circles or squares) the same size as the mousse. You need at least 16 good diamonds.
9.   To serve, take one chocolate diamond and place on the plate (after removing the cling film). Place a diamond of mousse on top, and top that with another chocolate diamond. Place 2 halves of an orange confit slice on the plate, and set the mousse on them. Flood the plate with the Grand Marnier crème anglaise, then garnish with a little citrus zest and 2 sprigs of mint.

CHAMPAGNE MOUSSE WITH WILD STRAWBERRIES

2 recipes Biscuit Cuillère (SEE PAGE 217)
325 ml (11 fl oz) champagne
4 gelatine leaves, soaked in cold water to soften
200 ml (7 fl oz) double cream

CHAMPAGNE JELLY

375 ml (13 fl oz) champagne
300 g (11 oz) caster sugar
4 gelatine leaves

SABAYON

75 g (2½ oz) caster sugar
200 ml (7 fl oz) Champagne
7 egg yolks

ITALIAN MERINGUE

125 g (4½ oz) caster sugar
90 ml (3 fl oz) water   egg whites

TO SERVE

50 g (2 oz) raspberries
about 175 g (6 oz) wild strawberries
a large handful of fresh mint
Confit of Citrus Zest (SEE PAGE 221)

1. Make the biscuit base first. Mix the ingredients together as in the recipe on page 217, then pour flat into a large baking tray lined with greased greaseproof paper. Smooth over, and bake in the preheated oven for 10 minutes. Remove from the oven and leave to cool in the tray. Turn out upside down, and remove the paper. Cut out to fit the base of 2 tart tins 25 cm (10 in) in diameter and 5 cm (2 in) deep.

2. Make the champagne syrup for the jelly. Bring the champagne to the boil with the sugar. Use a little of this to soak the biscuit bases in the tins. Keep the remaining syrup aside for later use.

3. To start the mousse itself, make the sabayon. Melt the sugar in the champagne, then boil to a syrup. Cool a little.

CHAMPAGNE MOUSSE WITH WILD STRAWBERRIES

4. Put the egg yolks in a bowl in a bain-marie, and pour in the syrup. Beat together over a gentle heat until the mixture thickens and a thermometer registers 83°C/181°F.

5. Take the bowl from the heat and continue beating until the sabayon is cold.

6. For the Italian meringue, put the sugar and water in a pan and heat to melt the sugar, then start to boil to 121°C/250°F, the hard ball stage (SEE BELOW).

7. When the syrup reaches 119°C/246°F, start to beat your egg whites in a mixer. When the syrup reaches 121°C/250°F, slowly pour it all into the egg whites, between beaters and side of bowl (to avoid spitting). Continue beating until the egg white is cold.

8. Place 50 ml (2 fl oz) of the champagne in a pan and add the softened gelatine. Heat very gently to melt the gelatine, but do not boil.

9. Lightly whip the cream and fold it together with the meringue. Then slowly fold in the sabayon. The folding must be done slowly to maintain the volume. Then whisk in the melted gelatine along with the remaining champagne. This is the basic mousse mixture, and it is now ready to set.

10. Scatter the raspberries over the soaked biscuit bases in the tins, and then pour in the mousse mixture. Smooth over, and leave to set in the fridge, about 12 hours.

11. A few hours before you want to serve, mix the remaining champagne syrup with the gelatine leaves which you have soaked beforehand, and melt. Cool over ice until thick and then spoon over the mousses in the tins. Leave to set to a thin layer of jelly.

12. To serve, cut the mousse and its biscuit base into the shape required - we serve in diamonds, but a wedge is less wasteful - and decorate with wild strawberries, mint, and citrus confit, pouring the coulis around.

CHEF'S NOTE

A complicated recipe, but one which is interesting to make for a very special party, and wonderful to eat.

Test for the hard ball stage by dropping a little of the syrup into iced water. Mould into a ball with the fingers and remove from the water. It should resist the fingers and still feel quite sticky.

8 PORTIONS

75 g (3 oz) caster sugar
5 egg yolks
2 vanilla pods
50 ml (2 fl oz) milk
450 ml (15 fl oz) double cream
demerara sugar

CRÈME BRÛLÉE
*WITH VANILLA
PODS*

1. Preheat the oven to 140°C/275°F/Gas 1.
2. Mix the sugar and egg yolks together well in a bowl.
3. Split the vanilla pods in half and scrape the seeds out into the milk and cream in a pan. Pour the cream and milk on to the yolks, mix well, then pass through a conical strainer to strain out the pods etc, but not the seeds.
4. Divide the mixture between 8 small, round, eared dishes or ramekin dishes, and cook in a bain-marie in the preheated oven for about 40 minutes. Allow to cool and set, then chill in the fridge.
5. Sprinkle the tops with the demerara sugar and glaze with a blow torch or under a hot grill. Allow the sugar to set hard. Serve in the dish.

4 PORTIONS

4 eggs
1 egg yolk
120 g (4½ oz) caster sugar
500 ml (17 fl oz) milk
1 drop vanilla essence
200 g (7 oz) Caramel (SEE PAGE 174)
50 g (2 oz) sultanas, soaked in a little dark rum

CRÈME CARAMEL
WITH SULTANAS

1. Preheat the oven to 140°C/275°F/Gas 1, and have ready 4 dariole moulds.
2. Mix the whole eggs, egg yolk and sugar together, then add the milk and vanilla essence. Pass through a fine sieve into a clean container.
3. Divide the caramel between the dariole moulds, then place the sultanas on the caramel.
4. Pour in the custard to the rim of the mould and cook in a bain-marie in the preheated oven for 40 minutes. Leave to cool.
5. To serve, turn out of the moulds on to the plates so that the caramel surrounds the sultana-topped shape.

CHEF'S NOTE
This was one of the specialities of the Box Tree when I worked there as a boy.

165

RASPBERRY SOUFFLÉ

4 PORTIONS

50 g (2 oz) unsalted butter
220 g (7¾ oz) caster sugar
16 fresh raspberries
100 ml (3½ fl oz) Framboise (raspberry eau de vie)
12 egg whites
200 ml (7 fl oz) Raspberry Reduction (SEE PAGE 219)

TO SERVE

1 recipe Raspberry Coulis (SEE PAGE 220)

1. Preheat the oven to 180°C/350°F/Gas 4, and grease 4 soufflé dishes, 7.5 cm (3 in) in diameter and 6.25 cm (2½ in) deep, well with half the butter. Place in the fridge until the butter sets hard, then butter again just before pouring in the soufflé mixture. Sprinkle with 20 g (¾ oz) of the caster sugar to coat, tipping out any excess.
2. Marinate the fresh raspberries in the Framboise until ready to use.
3. Put the egg whites into the bowl of your mixer and begin to beat. When they start to take shape, start adding the remaining sugar, a quarter at a time. When thoroughly mixed in, add another quarter and so on.
4. Put the raspberry reduction – the soufflé base – in a round bowl and whisk in a third of the beaten egg white; this loosens the base. Fold in the remaining egg white carefully.
5. Half fill the soufflé dishes with the mixture, then place 3 drained marinated raspberries in the centre. Fill to the top with the mixture then scrape off evenly with a palette knife. Run your finger around the edge to push the mixture away from the sides. Cook in the preheated oven for 10 minutes.
6. To serve, place the dish on a plate with a raspberry on top, and raspberry coulis on the side.

CHEF'S NOTE

Make a blackberry soufflé in exactly the same way, substituting blackberries for the raspberries (of course), and Crème de Cassis for the reduction and the marination. Use less water in the reduction – blackberries contain more than raspberries – and bake the soufflé for 7-8 minutes only instead of 10.

8 PORTIONS

40 g (1½ oz) cocoa powder
80 g (3¼ oz) plain flour
100 g (4 oz) caster sugar
500 ml (17 fl oz) milk
40 g (1½ oz) bitter chocolate, broken into pieces

TO FINISH AND SERVE

50 g (2 oz) unsalted butter
extra caster sugar and cocoa powder
icing sugar

CHOCOLATE SOUFFLÉ

1. Preheat the oven to 180°C/350°F/Gas 4, and prepare 8 soufflé dishes as in the previous recipe, dusting with some extra cocoa powder as well as extra sugar.

2. Sift the cocoa powder and the flour together, and add half the sugar.

3. Mix the remaining sugar with the milk and bring to the boil. Add to the dry ingredients. Whisk thoroughly, then blend in a processor until completely smooth.

4. Melt the chocolate in a bowl over a bain-marie, then add to the mixture.

5. Spoon 1½ tablespoons into each prepared soufflé dish, level off, and run your fingers around the edge to push the mixture away from the sides. Bake in the preheated oven for 10 minutes.

6. To serve, dust half the top with cocoa powder, the other half with icing sugar. Place the dish on a plate.

GRATIN D'AGRUMES, PASSIONFRUIT SORBET

6 PORTIONS

4 oranges
4 grapefruit
1 recipe Kirsch Sabayon (SEE PAGE 218)
6 Tuiles or Tulip Baskets (SEE PAGE 217)
6 sprigs mint
6 Spun Sugar cages (SEE PAGE 188)

PASSIONFRUIT SORBET

400 g (14 oz) passionfruit pulp (about 20-25 fruit)
200 ml (7 fl oz) fresh orange juice (2-3 oranges)
100 ml (3½ fl oz) Stock Syrup (SEE PAGE 220)

1. To make the sorbet, put the passionfruit pulp, seeds and their juice into a pan. Add about 1½ tablespoons water and cook gently for about 5 minutes over a low heat.

2. Liquidise the mixture for 30 seconds – no longer, or the seeds will be ground finely and will discolour the mixture. Push through a sieve a few times.

3. Mix the sieved pulp with the orange juice and stock syrup. Check the flavour and add a little extra sugar if needed. Churn in an ice-cream machine until frozen, or freeze in the freezer.

4. Segment the oranges and grapefruit, then keep aside on a dry cloth. Confit the zest of the fruit (SEE PAGE 221).

5. When ready to serve, place the citrus segments around the plate with a little zest, pour the sabayon over them, and then grill for a few minutes to lightly brown.

6. To serve, and working quickly, place a tuile in the centre of each plate, fill with a scoop of sorbet, and garnish with some citrus zest and mint. Top with a sugar cage.

CHEF'S NOTE

To make cages from spun sugar, criss-cross the sugar threads over the back of an oiled ladle to weave a semi-circle. Trim the bases and cool. Handle very carefully.

170

6 PORTIONS

200 g (7 oz) unsalted butter, melted
8-10 slices white bread
300 ml (10 fl oz) milk
300 ml (10 fl oz) double cream
a pinch of salt
1 vanilla pod, split lengthways
5 eggs
40 g (1½ oz) caster sugar
60 g (2¼ oz) sultanas

TO SERVE

½ recipe Crème Anglaise (SEE PAGE 219)

BREAD AND BUTTER PUDDING

1. Preheat the oven to 140°C/275°F/Gas 1, and use a little of the melted butter to grease a dish 25 x 25 cm (10 x 10 in) and 5 cm (2 in) deep.
2. Dip the bread into the melted butter and place it in the buttered dish.
3. Bring the milk, cream and salt to the boil together with the split vanilla pod.
4. Whisk together the eggs and sugar, and add to the milk and cream mixture.
5. Pour this custard through a fine sieve over the bread in the dish and sprinkle the sultanas on top.
6. Cook in the preheated oven in a bain-marie for approximately an hour.
7. To serve, cut out into good sized portions, using a knife or circular pastry cutter, and serve warm with cold or warm crème anglaise.

CHEF'S NOTE

This is one of my very favourite puddings. When it contains a lot of fruit, it's fantastic. It must be eaten warm, though, never cold.

4 PORTIONS

4 large Cox's apples
200 g (7 oz) Mincemeat (SEE PAGE 221)

CINNAMON ICE CREAM (15 portions)

10 egg yolks
200 g (7 oz) caster sugar
50 ml (2 fl oz) glucose syrup
700 ml (1⅕ pints) milk
250 ml (8 fl oz) double cream
2 cinnamon sticks

CARAMEL

150 g (5 oz) caster sugar
50 ml (2 fl oz) water

TO SERVE

4 Tuiles or Tulip Baskets (SEE PAGE 217)
chocolate shavings (use a potato peeler or cheese slice)

1. Make the ice cream first. Mix the egg yolks, sugar and glucose syrup together well in a rounded bowl.
2. Put the milk, cream and cinnamon sticks in a pan and bring to the boil.
3. Pour the hot liquid over the yolk mixture and mix well. Return to the pan and the heat, and cook very slowly until the mixture thickens enough to coat the back of the spoon.
4. Remove from the heat and pass through a fine sieve into a bowl over ice to cool it down quickly. When cold, put in an ice-cream machine and churn until frozen, or freeze in the freezer.
5. Preheat the oven to 180°C/350°F/Gas 4.
6. To prepare the apples, peel, core and fill each one with the mincemeat.
7. For the caramel, boil the sugar and water together until golden brown and caramel coloured.
8. Place the apples on a baking tray and coat each with the caramel. Place the tray in the preheated oven and bake until the apples are cooked thoroughly without losing their shape, about 25-30 minutes, depending on size.
9. To serve, place a baked apple on each plate, on top of some caramel and juices. Serve a good-sized scoop of cinnamon ice cream in a tulip basket next to the apple. Decorate the ice cream with chocolate shavings (which look like cinnamon quills!)

8 PORTIONS

1 x 20 cm (8 in) Sweet Pastry Tart Case *(SEE PAGE 216)*
apricot jam

POACHED PEARS

5 pears, peeled and cored
1 litre (1¾ pints) water
350 g (12 oz) caster sugar
4 vanilla pods, split

CRÈME D'AMANDE

250 g (9 oz) unsalted butter, softened
250 g (9 oz) caster sugar
250 g (9 oz) ground almonds
3 eggs
50 g (2 oz) plain flour

TO SERVE

1 recipe Poire William Crème Anglaise *(SEE PAGE 219)*

TARTE BOURDALOUE

1. Preheat the oven to 160°C/325°F/Gas 3.
2. For the poached pears, bring the water, sugar and vanilla pods to the boil together in a suitable pan, then add the pears. Poach until the pears become soft but not mushy. Place the pears on a dry cloth to drain. Halve them lengthways.
3. To make the crème d'amande, combine the soft butter with the sugar and ground almonds. Slowly beat in the eggs. Make sure the mixture does not separate. Finally fold in the flour.
4. Pipe the crème d'amande into the blind-baked pastry case to come three-quarters up the height of the case. Arrange the pear halves, flat side down, in this.
5. Cook in the preheated oven for 30-40 minutes.
6. To serve, trim the edges of the pastry, and glaze the top of the tart with apricot jam. Cut the tart into 8 portions. Serve warm with Poire William crème anglaise on the side.

CHOCOLATE TART

500 g (18 oz) Valhrona Equatorial chocolate, broken into pieces
3 eggs
200 ml (7 fl oz) milk
350 ml (12 fl oz) double cream
1 x 20 cm (8 in) Sweet Pastry Tart Case (SEE PAGE 216)

TO SERVE

chocolate shavings (use a potato peeler or cheese slice)
icing sugar

1. Preheat the oven to 180°C/350°F/Gas 4.
2. Melt the chocolate in a bowl over a bain-marie; this should not be too warm.
3. Whisk the eggs together in a large bowl.
4. Bring the milk and cream to the boil in a pan, then pour on to the eggs, and whisk together.
5. Pass through a sieve on to the chocolate and mix well. Pour this into the blind-baked tart case.
6. Put the tart into the oven, and immediately turn the oven off. Leave the tart in the oven for 40-45 minutes.
7. When cool, trim the edges of the pastry, and cut the tart into 10 portions. Serve with chocolate shavings on the top, and sprinkled with icing sugar.

4 PORTIONS

300 g (11 oz) Puff Pastry (SEE PAGE 215)
500 g (18 oz) rhubarb
200 g (7 oz) unsalted butter, melted
200 g (7 oz) caster sugar
½ recipe Crème Anglaise (SEE PAGE 219)

VANILLA ICE CREAM (10 portions)

6 egg yolks   120 g (4½ oz) caster sugar
500 ml (17 fl oz) milk   6 vanilla pods, split
200 ml (7 fl oz) double cream

RHUBARB TART
WITH VANILLA ICE CREAM

1. Make the ice cream first. Mix the egg yolks and sugar together well in a bowl.
2. Put the milk, the vanilla pods and scraped-out seeds in a pan and bring to the boil.
3. Pour the hot liquid over the yolk mixture and mix well. Return the mixture to the pan and to the heat, and cook very slowly, stirring, until the mixture thickens.
4. Remove from the heat and pass through a fine sieve into a bowl over ice to cool it down quickly. When cold, whip in the whipped cream. Put in an ice-cream machine and churn until frozen, or freeze in the freezer.
5. Preheat the oven to 180°C/350°F/Gas 4.
6. Roll out the puff pastry to a circle 25 cm (10 in) in diameter, then pleat the pastry all the way around the edge. Leave to rest.
7. To prepare the rhubarb, slice very thinly widthways, and arrange carefully and neatly on top of the pastry base, making sure there are no gaps.
8. Brush the melted butter over the tart, then sprinkle with the caster sugar.
9. Place the tart on a tray and cook in the preheated oven for 1 hour. Half-way through the cooking, place another baking tray on top of the tart, and invert the tart on to it, rhubarb side down. Return to the oven to cook, to make sure the rhubarb is nicely caramelised.
10. To serve, cut in wedges, and accompany with a scoop of vanilla ice cream and the crème anglaise.

CHEF'S NOTE

You can make this tart with apples, bananas or pears as well. Use only 150 g (5 oz) sugar, as these fruits are not so sour as rhubarb.

TARTE NORMANDE

8 PORTIONS

400 g (14 oz) Puff Pastry (SEE PAGE 215)
12 medium apples (Cox's)
250 g (9 oz) unsalted butter
250 g (9 oz) caster sugar

CUSTARD

40 g (1½ oz) caster sugar
3 small egg yolks
1 vanilla pod
25 ml (1 fl oz) milk
225 ml (7½ fl oz) double cream

TO SERVE

2 recipes Caramel Sauce (SEE PAGE 218)
Calvados to taste
8 scoops Vanilla Ice Cream (SEE PAGE 181)

1. Roll out the pastry and use to line a 25 cm (10 in) tart tin. Chill for half an hour.
2. Preheat the oven to 180°C/350°F/Gas 4.
3. Blind-bake the tart case in the preheated oven as on page 216. Remove from the oven, and leave in the tin to cool. Reduce the temperature of the oven to 160°C/325°F/Gas 3.
4. Make the custard as in the Crème Brûlée recipe on page 163, but caramelise the sugar first before mixing with the egg yolks and other ingredients.
5. Peel and core the apples. Cut 4 of them into slices and mix with a little of the butter and sugar; cook to a purée. Push through a sieve, and keep to one side. Cut the remaining apples into 10 slices each.
6. Heat the remaining butter and the sugar together to a caramel, and then nicely caramelise the apple wedges.
7. Put the purée on the bottom of the cooked tart case, smooth, and arrange the caramelised wedges of apple neatly on top.
8. Pass the custard through a conical strainer into the tart case to come three-quarters of the way up the sides.
9. Place in the reduced temperature oven and bake for 30-40 minutes. It will not be fully set. Allow to cool to room temperature.
10. To serve, slice very carefully, and serve in wedges with some Calvados flavoured caramel sauce and a scoop of vanilla ice cream.

16 PORTIONS

CHOCOLATE ROULADE

7 eggs, separated
200 g (7 oz) caster sugar
50 g (2 oz) cocoa powder

CHOCOLATE MOUSSE

315 g (11¼ oz) soft unsalted butter
150 g (5 oz) cocoa powder
550 ml (18 fl oz) double cream
60 g (2¼ oz) icing sugar
150 g (5 oz) bitter chocolate, broken into pieces
8 egg yolks
275 g (10 oz) caster sugar

TO FINISH AND SERVE

12 After Eight mints
white chocolate curls (or shavings)
4 recipes Caramel Sauce (SEE PAGE 218)
extra cocoa powder and icing sugar

MARQUISE DE CHOCOLAT,
CARAMEL SAUCE

1. Preheat the oven to 200°C/400°F/Gas 6, and have ready a 40 x 60 cm (16 x 24 in) non-stick baking tray.

2. To make the chocolate roulade, mix the egg yolks, 70 g (2¾ oz) of the sugar and the cocoa powder together. Do not over mix.

3. Whisk the egg whites until stiff, and gradually whisk in the remaining sugar. Continue beating until stiff and glossy.

4. Gently fold the meringue into the yolk mixture until smooth. Spread on to the non-stick tray and bake in the preheated oven for 10 minutes. Remove and allow to get cold. Cover with a cloth.

5. To make the chocolate mousse, melt the butter gently with the cocoa powder in a bain-marie.

6. Whisk the cream with the icing sugar to the ribbon stage - when the lifted beater leaves a ribbon trail on the surface.

7. Melt the chocolate in a bain-marie. Cool a little.

8. Whisk the egg yolks and caster sugar together until thick, then fold in the melted chocolate followed by first the butter mix, then the cream. Do not over mix as this may cause the mixture to split. Chill.

9. Line a terrine 25 x 8 cm (10 x 3¼ in) and 7 cm (2¾ in) deep with silicone paper (base and sides). Cut the chocolate roulade into rectangles that will fit the terrine; you will need 4.

10. Put the chocolate mousse into a piping bag, and pipe a layer into the bottom of the lined terrine - use about a quarter. Place a layer of chocolate roulade on top. Repeat this once more, then make a layer of the After Eight mints. Pipe in the mousse, and top with roulade twice more. You will have four layers each of mousse and roulade, and one of mints (which add an unexpected flavour and crunch). Cover with foil, then chill to set, or freeze.

11. To serve, turn the terrine out of the mould, and cut into thin slices. Place on a plate and decorate with chocolate curls. Pour the cold caramel sauce around, and dust lightly with icing sugar and cocoa powder.

CHEF'S NOTE

This recipe may seem very complicated, consisting of many elements, but it freezes very well, so can be made in advance of your special occasion. It needs 3 hours at least in the fridge to come round after freezing, and then you can bring it to room temperature as you start your main course.

OPÉRA

A complicated dish, but again it is very special, and freezes well.

ABOUT 12 GOOD PORTIONS
1 recipe Chocolate Roulade (SEE PAGE 183)

KAHLUA SYRUP

250 ml (8 fl oz) water
250 g (9 oz) caster sugar
50 ml (2 fl oz) strong espresso coffee
20 ml (¾ fl oz) Kahlua (coffee liqueur)

CHOCOLATE GANACHE

500 g (18 oz) good dark chocolate
500 ml (17 fl oz) double cream

COFFEE BUTTER CREAM

2 egg yolks
2 eggs
375 g (13 oz) caster sugar
100 ml (3½ fl oz) water
400 g (14 oz) unsalted butter
20 g (¾ oz) instant coffee powder

TO SERVE

1 recipe Coffee Crème Anglaise (SEE PAGE 219)

1. Make the chocolate roulade as described on page 183. Leave to cool.
2. Make the syrup by melting the sugar in the water, and boiling to 125°C/257°F. Add the coffee and Kahlua.
3. To make the chocolate ganache, break the chocolate into a metal bowl. Bring the cream to the boil in a separate pan, and add to the chocolate. Mix until smooth and melted.
4. To make the coffee butter cream, whip the egg yolks and eggs to the ribbon stage - when the lifted beater leaves a ribbon trail on the surface.
5. Melt the sugar in the water and boil to the soft ball stage - when a drop of the syrup moulded into a ball in iced water loses its shape when taken out of the water. (Using a sugar thermometer, when it registers 117°C/243°F.)

186

6. Add the sugar syrup to the eggs and whisk until cold.

7. Whisk in the soft butter, then add the instant coffee dissolved in a tiny amount of water.

8. To assemble, cut the chocolate roulade into three equal pieces. Trim if necessary. Moisten these with the Kahlua syrup.

9. Spread half the soft chocolate ganache evenly over one of the moistened roulade pieces, and set in the fridge.

10. Place the second layer of roulade over the ganache and spread with half of the coffee butter cream. Place the third layer of roulade on top, and spread with the remaining coffee butter cream. Do this as evenly as possible. Set in the fridge for 20 minutes.

11. Spread the remaining ganache on top of the coffee butter cream, again as evenly as possible, as this is the final layer of the opéra.

12. To serve, cut the opéra into the required slices, and serve with the coffee crème anglaise. It is best at room temperature.

CHEF'S NOTE

This is another tricky and complicated dish, and another use for the chocolate roulade. It's very rich and delicious, and like the Marquise de Chocolat it freezes well — so you can make it well in advance. But remember to unfreeze it for at least three hours in the fridge, and then bring it to room temperature for about another half an hour.

OEUFS À LA NEIGE

8 PORTIONS

4 egg whites
70 g (2¾ oz) caster sugar
500 ml (17 fl oz) milk
1 recipe Crème Anglaise (SEE PAGE 219)
made with the above milk

SPUN SUGAR

100 g (4 oz) caster sugar
2 tablespoons glucose syrup
2 tablespoons water

1. Whip the egg whites for the meringue until stiff, then beat the sugar in gradually.
2. Scald the milk by bringing to the boil in a shallow wide pan.
3. Drop the meringue mixture from a tablespoon in rounds on to the milk. Poach gently without letting the milk boil for about 4 minutes, turning them once. Lift them out carefully with a skimmer on to a towel.
4. Make the crème anglaise in the usual way (SEE PAGE 219), but using the meringue poaching milk. When ready, remove from the heat, and pour through a sieve into your serving bowl or bowls (soup plates are best). Leave to cool.
5. When the crème anglaise is cold, place the meringues on top. Chill before serving.
6. For the spun sugar, mix the caster sugar, glucose syrup and water in a pan, and melt slowly before boiling until the mixture becomes golden brown, the hard crack stage, see below. Remove from the heat and dip the base of the saucepan into a bowl of cold water to stop further cooking. Leave the caramel to cool slightly, then dip a fork into it and flick the trailing threads of caramel over a rolling pin. Carefully make a loose ball of spun sugar. Repeat until you have eight balls in total.
7. To serve, place each ball on top of the oeufs à la neige.

CHEF'S NOTE

Test for hard crack stage by dipping a teaspoon into cold water and then into the syrup and then back into the cold water again. When the resulting cooled sugar ceases to be pliable and cracks like glass, it is ready. Test very frequently as the syrup moves from one stage to the next in a matter of seconds. If using a sugar thermometer, it should register 149-154°C/300-310°F.

188

SAUCES & ACCOMPANIMENTS

ERE ARE THE STOCKS, sauces, vegetable accompaniments, flavour enhancers, garnishes and decorations that are vital for at least one dish in this book. A few you will have seen before, since inevitably the classic recipes, or the recipes which are central to *my* way of cooking, are the same as in my previous books.

Good stocks are important to good soups and sauces, and I would always recommend that the domestic kitchen should have some available, in fridge or freezer. However, ready-prepared stocks can now be found in some supermarkets, and they can be used *in extremis*.

Reductions of stocks form the basis of most sauces, and I think, if you work your way through a number of the sauce pages following, you will grasp how simple, in essence, many classical sauces are. What you want in a sauce is *taste*, and by reducing a flavoured liquid – a stock or an alcohol, or both – you *concentrate* taste. If you then add a little cream or swirl in a few dice of butter, you will have something that is very special.

Our vegetable accompaniments and garnishes are fairly basic and simple, but they too, like the sauces, add taste as well as an enormous amount of textural interest. We've suggested possible accompaniments in each main-course recipe, but there is a wide variety of choices here, if you fancied something else. For instance, we serve pomme fondant with roasts, but there's nothing wrong with the traditional way, putting the potatoes in the pan with the roast, to get that crunchy bit on the bottom. And any vegetable can be cooked as we do them, not by boiling, but by blanching them and finishing them in an emulsion of butter and stock or water. You can even do this to frozen sprouts or peas, and no-one will know the difference!

CHICKEN STOCK

We use this 'single-cooked' chicken stock in juice-based sauces, as well as in soups. The recipe should be used as a basis for other poultry stocks - duck, guinea fowl, etc.

MAKES ABOUT 4.5 LITRES (8 PINTS)

2.75 kg (6 lb) raw chicken carcasses, chopped
about 5.75 litres (10 pints) cold water
3 celery stalks
1 leek   1 large onion   2 carrots
½ whole head of garlic

1.   Place the raw chicken carcasses in a large pot, then cover with cold water. Bring to the boil, then skim.
2.   Keep the vegetables whole, but peel them if necessary. Tie the celery and leek together with string – this prevents them breaking up, which helps to clarify the stock.

3.   Add all the vegetables and the garlic to the pot, then bring back to the boil. Skim, then leave to simmer, uncovered, for 4 hours.
4.   Pass through a fine sieve. The stock should be a light amber colour, and clear. Store in the fridge for a couple of days, or freeze (but for no longer than 3 months).

We use this 'twice-cooked' chicken stock in cream-based sauces, where it compensates for the diminution of flavour.

DOUBLE CHICKEN STOCK

MAKES ABOUT 1 LITRE (1¾ PINTS)

900 g (2 lb) chicken winglets
2 tablespoons olive oil
1 large carrot, chopped   1 celery stalk, chopped
½ large onion   the white of 1 leek
½ whole head of garlic
1.5 litres (2½ pints) Chicken Stock (see above)
1 bay leaf   1 sprig thyme   3 sprigs parsley

1.   Chop each winglet into three or four pieces and cook half of them in half the oil, without colouring.
2.   Peel and trim the vegetables as appropriate. Cut into small dice (*mirepoix*). Peel and finely chop the garlic.
3.   Separately cook the *mirepoix* vegetables, plus the garlic, in the remaining oil, without colouring.

4.   Add the *mirepoix* to the cooked winglets, add the raw winglets, then cover with the chicken stock. Bring to the boil and skim.
5.   Add the bay leaf, thyme and parsley and simmer for about 1 hour.
6.   Pass through a fine sieve lined with muslin. The stock should be an amber colour. Keep in the fridge for up to a week, or freeze (but for no longer than 3 months).

You can make a sauce for lamb from the stock below. Allow about 120-150 ml (4-5 fl oz) stock per person, place in a small saucepan and boil to reduce by half. Add a sprig of herb relevant to the dish being prepared, and leave to infuse for 10 minutes or so. Then heat through briefly, add a small knob of butter and season to taste. Strain.

LAMB STOCK/SAUCE

MAKES ABOUT 1.5 LITRES (2½ PINTS)

2.25 kg (5 lb) raw lamb bones
2 tablespoons vegetable oil
1 onion   1 celery stalk   1 carrot   1 leek
2½ tablespoons Tomato Fondue (SEE PAGE 206)
1 whole head of garlic, cloves peeled
1.5 litres (2½ pints) Veal Stock (SEE PAGE 192)
1 litre (1¾ pints) Chicken Stock (SEE PAGE 190)
500 ml (17 fl oz) water   1 bay leaf   1 sprig thyme

1.   Chop the lamb bones very finely, then roast them in 1 tablespoon of the oil in a tray on top of the stove until golden brown. Drain well.
2.   Prepare the vegetables as appropriate, then cut into dice. Sweat in the remaining oil on top of the stove. Do not colour them.
3.   Add the tomato fondue and the peeled garlic, and cook to a 'jam'. Add the lamb bones.
4.   Bring the two stocks to the boil in a separate pan, and pour over the bones to cover.

Bring back to the boil and add the cold water. Skim the fat off thoroughly.
5.   Add the herbs and cook the stock at a fast simmer for 1 hour, skimming regularly. It will reduce down to about 1.5 litres (2½ pints).
6.   Pass through a sieve, then through muslin six times to ensure that it is clear. Cool and store, or freeze, or use in a sauce (see above).

VEAL STOCK

Veal stock is used by many professional cooks, primarily because it gives a sauce so much more body - due to the gelatine in the young bones. You can, of course, halve the recipe. You can also use this recipe to make a beef stock: substitute beef knuckle and skirt for the veal.

MAKES ABOUT 3 LITRES (5¼ PINTS)

2.75 kg (6 lb) veal knuckle bones
120 ml (4 fl oz) olive oil
1 onion, peeled and chopped
3 carrots, chopped
3 celery stalks, chopped
½ whole head of garlic, cloves peeled
4 tablespoons tomato purée
450 g (1 lb) button mushrooms, thinly sliced
¼ bottle Madeira
10 litres (17½ pints) hot water
1 sprig thyme   1 bay leaf

1.   Cook the veal knuckle bones in 4 table-spoons of the oil until golden brown, stirring and turning occasionally.
2.   Simultaneously, in a separate pan, cook the onion, carrot, celery, and garlic in 2 table-spoons of the oil until golden brown, without burning.
3.   Add the tomato purée to the vegetables, stir in and allow to gently and lightly colour. Be careful not to burn at this stage.
4.   In a separate pan, colour the button mush-rooms in the remaining oil, then deglaze the pan with the Madeira. Boil to reduce down to almost nothing. Add the syrupy mushrooms to the rest of the vegetables.
5.   When the veal bones are golden brown, place in a large stock pot and cover with the hot water. Bring to the boil and skim.
6.   Add the vegetables and herbs to the bones and bring back to the boil. Skim, then allow to simmer for 8-12 hours, topping up with water to keep the bones covered as and when required.
7.   Pass through a fine sieve into another, preferably tall, pan, and boil to reduce by half. Cool, then store in the fridge for up to a week, or freeze (but for no longer than 3 months).

FISH STOCK

The best bones to use are turbot or Dover sole, although monkfish is good too. Use the stock for poaching fish, or in fish sauces or soups.

MAKES ABOUT 2 LITRES (3½ PINTS)

1.8 kg (4 lb) fish bones
white of 2 small leeks, finely chopped
1 large celery stalk, finely chopped
½ onion, peeled and finely chopped
½ fennel bulb, finely chopped
½ whole head of garlic, cloves peeled
1 tablespoon olive oil
200 ml (7 fl oz) white wine
2 litres (3½ pints) water
1 lemon, sliced   2 sprigs parsley

1. Wash the fish bones very thoroughly, and chop up.
2. Cook the chopped vegetables and garlic in the oil for a few minutes to soften, but without colouring them.
3. Add the fish bones and white wine and cook, without colouring (the bones will turn white), for about 5 more minutes, then boil for a few minutes to reduce the wine a little.

4. Add the water, bring to the boil and skim well.
5. Add the sliced lemon and parsley, then simmer for 20 minutes.
6. Pass through a sieve and leave to cool. Store in the fridge for a day only, or freeze (but for no longer than a month).

A stock made from scallop trimmings always makes the best sauce for scallops. Never throw scallop skirts away as they are so full of flavour that can be utilised in a stock. To make into a sauce, reduce 150 ml (5 fl oz) stock per person by half, then add 1 tablespoon double cream, a teaspoon unsalted butter, and lemon juice, salt and pepper to taste. Whisk up with a little hand blender.

Always get your fishmonger to trim and clean fish and shellfish, but take the trimmings home with you and use to make a stock or sauce (or freeze for future use). When cooking shellfish, keep their poaching liquor and add it to a fish stock.

SCALLOP STOCK

.MAKES ABOUT 2 LITRES (3½ PINTS)

18 scallop skirts, well cleaned
1 carrot, finely chopped   1 celery stalk, finely chopped
1 small leek, finely chopped
1 tablespoon olive oil
2 litres (3½ pints) Fish Stock (SEE PAGE 192), or water

1. Cook the vegetables in the oil for a few minutes to soften, without colouring.
2. Add the scallop skirts and cook for a few minutes more, without colouring.
3. Add the fish stock or water, bring to the boil and skim.

4. Cook for 20 minutes, then pass through a muslin-lined sieve, and leave to cool. Store in the fridge for about a day, or freeze (but for no longer than a month).

This is used in soups.

VEGETABLE STOCK

MAKES ABOUT 900 ML (1½ PINTS)

2 courgettes
4 onions, peeled
1 fennel bulb
2 leeks
8 garlic cloves, peeled and crushed
14 white peppercorns
50 g (2 oz) unsalted butter
1.2 litres (2 pints) cold water
15 g (½ oz) each of chopped chervil, basil and tarragon

1. Coarsely chop the vegetables. Sweat them in the butter in a large saucepan with the garlic and peppercorns until soft.
2. Add just enough cold water to cover, and bring to the boil. Skim and simmer for 15 minutes.

3. Add the herbs and cook for another 2 minutes only. Strain immediately. Keep any excess in a covered container in the fridge for a couple of days at most, or freeze.

MADEIRA JELLY

This makes a very flavourful jelly to accompany the terrine on page 49, but it can also be used as a consommé or broth. Do not reduce as you would for the jelly, then to the hot broth add herbs, wild mushrooms or vegetable dice to taste. This makes a huge amount of liquid, but it keeps well in the freezer.

MAKES ABOUT 3 LITRES (5¼ PINTS)

1 shin of veal, chopped into osso buco
1 shin of beef, cut similarly
1 boiling fowl, chopped into small joints
1 calf's foot, split
2 onions   2 large carrots, split lengthways
2 celery stalks   2 leeks   1 head of garlic, cut in half
1 bouquet garni   1 bottle Madeira
500 ml (17 fl oz) soy sauce   10 litres (17½ pints) water

1. Put the meats into a large stock pot along with all the remaining ingredients, and bring to the boil. Skim very well, and cook, uncovered, for 2½ hours. The liquid must barely simmer, so that it stays clear; the heat, therefore, must be very low.
2. Pass gently through muslin into another pan: the liquid should be totally clear and amber in colour. It can now be used for a broth or consommé, and it will not need salting because of the soy.
3. Reduce by half by simmering to create the jelly. It will be intensely flavoured. Leave to set in dishes, or in one or two shallow trays. Serve it smooth, if you like, or chop finely and pipe or spoon for decoration.

MADEIRA SAUCE

Store this sauce — which is good with poultry and beef — in a covered bowl in the refrigerator until required. It can also be frozen.

4 PORTIONS

1 tablespoon vegetable oil
100 g (4 oz) pie veal, chopped
3 shallots, peeled and finely sliced
40 g (1½ oz) mushrooms, sliced
2 large garlic cloves, peeled and sliced in half
1 small sprig thyme   ¼ bay leaf
1 tablespoon sherry vinegar   1 tablespoon Cognac
325 ml (11 fl oz) Madeira
325 ml (11 fl oz) Veal Stock (SEE PAGE 192)
75 ml (2½ fl oz) Chicken Stock (SEE PAGE 190)
50 ml (2 fl oz) water

1. Heat the oil in a large frying pan over a moderate heat and sauté the meat for about 10 minutes, turning it occasionally, until golden brown all over.
2. Add the shallot, mushrooms, garlic, thyme and bay leaf, and continue to cook for about 5 minutes, stirring frequently, until all the liquid from the mushrooms has gone.
3. Add the vinegar and continue to cook until the liquid has evaporated, then deglaze with the Cognac, pouring it around the outside of the pan. Pour in the Madeira and cook rapidly to reduce it by about four-fifths.
4. Add the stock and the water, stir and bring to the boil. Reduce the heat and simmer for 20 minutes, removing any scum that appears from time to time. Pass through a muslin-lined sieve three times, rinsing the muslin each time.

This is a jus which can be made with either chicken or lamb. It is virtually an essence of chicken or lamb. Serve it with poultry or game birds when made with chicken, with lamb and other red meats when made with lamb.

JUS RÔTI

8 PORTIONS

6 chicken legs (or 1 shoulder of lamb)
olive oil
200 ml (7 fl oz) water
200 ml (7 fl oz) Chicken Stock (SEE PAGE 190)
200 ml (7 fl oz) Veal Stock (SEE PAGE 192)

1. Preheat the oven to 140°C/275°F/Gas 1 and roast the chicken (or lamb) for 1½-2 hours. Use a very little oil in the tray.
2. Remove from the oven and add the water and stocks to the roasting tray. Bring quickly to the boil, then remove the chicken (or lamb) from the liquid. Place on a rack over the liquid.
3. Wrap the chicken legs (or lamb) tightly with cling film on the top, and then squeeze so that all the essential juices drip into the liquid in the roasting tray.
4. Discard the meats (or feed them to a dog or cat), and reduce the liquid to concentrate the flavour.

The reductions for this basic red wine sauce can be prepared in advance. It can then be finished with the butter at the last moment. It is good served with eggs, fish, poultry, meat or game; use a stock appropriate to the main ingredient - fish stock for fish, chicken stock for poultry etc.

RED WINE SAUCE

4 PORTIONS

500 ml (17 fl oz) red wine   100 ml (3½ fl oz) port
500 ml (17 fl oz) chosen stock
50 g (2 oz) hard unsalted butter, diced

1. Pour the red wine and port into a suitable saucepan and boil to reduce by one-third.
2. Boil the stock down to reduce it to a good coating consistency, when it lightly coats the back of a wooden spoon.
3. Add the red wine and port reduction and the butter dice, and allow to melt in.

195

JUNIPER JUS

This is served with Roast Saddle of Lamb, the recipe on page 130.

Reduce the red wine and port as above, then mix with 2 stock reduction, but using half and half of lamb and beef stocks (SEE PAGES 191, 192). Add 20 crushed juniper berries, cover with cling film, and leave to infuse for at least 10 minutes. Melt in the butter as above, and then pass through muslin or a fine sieve. You could leave a few whole juniper berries in the sauce if liked.

SAUCE DIABLE

This is the ideal sauce to serve with offal, especially calf's liver. The diable reduction below will make more than you need for this sauce, but it keeps well in the fridge.

8 PORTIONS

900 g (2 lb) chicken winglets, chopped
50 ml (2 fl oz) vegetable oil
4 shallots, peeled and sliced
2 garlic cloves, peeled and sliced
100 g (4 oz) button mushrooms, sliced
1 sprig thyme   1 bay leaf
25 g (1 oz) white peppercorns, crushed
200 ml (7 fl oz) Diable Reduction (see below)
400 ml (14 fl oz) Chicken Stock (SEE PAGE 190)
600 ml (1 pint) Beef Stock (SEE PAGE 192)

DIABLE REDUCTION

250 ml (9 fl oz) white wine
250 ml (9 fl oz) white wine vinegar
15 white peppercorns, crushed
1 small sprig thyme   1 bay leaf
5 shallots, peeled and sliced

TO FINISH

100 g (4 oz) shallots, peeled and finely diced
50 g (2 oz) unsalted butter

1. For the diable reduction, bring all the ingredients to the boil in a suitable pan, and cook for 20 minutes. Rest, then strain out the solids.
2. Caramelise and brown the chopped chicken winglets in the oil. When golden, pour the oil off through a colander.
3. Put the chicken winglets back into the pan, add the sliced shallot and garlic, and cook until golden.
4. Add the mushrooms, thyme and bay leaf, and cook for a few more minutes.
5. Add the peppercorns and measured diable reduction, and simmer for 5 minutes.
6. Pour in the stocks and bring to the boil, skimming off any impurities. Simmer for 30 minutes, then pass through muslin.
7. Reduce by boiling until of a good coating consistency.
8. Meanwhile, cook the shallot dice in half the butter to soften. Dice the remaining butter.
9. Finish the sauce by adding the shallot and butter dice. Mix and melt in.

196

This goes well with the Confit de Canard recipe on page 113, and the ham on page 128.

4 PORTIONS

2 shallots, unpeeled
1 carrot, unpeeled   1 celery stalk
100 ml (3½ fl oz) vegetable oil
50 g (2 oz) brown sugar
100 ml (3½ fl oz) port   200 ml (7 fl oz) red wine
150 ml (5 fl oz) Chicken Stock (SEE PAGE 190)
150 ml (5 fl oz) Veal Stock (SEE PAGE 192)
50 g (2 oz) hard unsalted butter, diced

BITTERSWEET PORT WINE SAUCE

1.   Roughly chop the shallots, carrot and celery, and fry in the oil until they appear to be burned. This is the vegetable sugars caramelising, and will contribute to the bittersweet flavour.
2.   Add the sugar, and caramelise further, but lightly.

3.   Add the port and red wine and boil to reduce down to about 100 ml (3½ fl oz).
4.   Add the stocks and again reduce down, this time to a coating consistency.
5.   Pass through a chinois sieve, then melt in the butter dice.

This is served with tuna; see page 100.

4 PORTIONS

3 shallots, peeled and sliced
1 garlic clove, peeled and halved
100 g (4 oz) unsalted butter
120 ml (4 fl oz) port   250 ml (8 fl oz) red wine
50 ml (2 fl oz) red wine vinegar
50 g (2 oz) caster sugar
150 ml (5 fl oz) Veal Stock (SEE PAGE 192)

SAUCE AIGRE-DOUX

1.   Sweat the shallot and garlic in half of the butter to soften.
2.   Add the port, red wine and vinegar, and boil to reduce down to about 150 ml (5 fl oz).

3.   Caramelise the sugar in a clean pan, then mix in the port reduction and veal stock.
4.   Add the remaining butter in pieces, melt in, then pass through a fine sieve.

This is particularly good with the pigeon on page 121. It can be made at least a day in advance.

4 PORTIONS

225 g (8 oz) chicken winglets
100 ml (3½ fl oz) olive oil
4 shallots   2 celery stalks   1 carrot   1 white of leek
4 tablespoons Tomato Fondue (SEE PAGE 206)
500 ml (17 fl oz) Double Chicken Stock (SEE PAGE 191)
1 bay leaf   3 sprigs thyme

JUS OF THYME

197

1.   Chop the chicken winglets and brown in the oil in a large pan. Remove using a slotted spoon.

2.   Trim, peel and roughly chop all the vegetables. Caramelise and brown them in the oil remaining in the chicken pan.

3.   Add the tomato fondue to the vegetables and cook, stirring constantly, to mix all well together.

4.   Add the browned winglets, the stock, and enough water to cover. Bring to the boil, then add the bay leaf and 2 sprigs of the thyme, and leave to cook slowly for 20-30 minutes.

5.   Pass through a sieve then boil to reduce the liquid by half.

6.   Add the remaining thyme leaves at the last minute and allow to infuse for a few minutes before straining - if you like - and serving.

LIME JUS

We serve this sauce with calf's liver at The Canteen, adding a little extra lime juice at the last moment.

8 PORTIONS

4 shallots, peeled and finely chopped
1 tomato, skinned, seeded and chopped
1 garlic clove, peeled and crushed
1 teaspoon caster sugar
½ bay leaf   75 g (3 oz) unsalted butter
20 ml (¾ fl oz) sherry vinegar   juice of 2 limes
100 ml (3½ fl oz) port   300 ml (10 fl oz) Noilly Prat
200 ml (7 fl oz) Chicken Stock (SEE PAGE 190)
300 ml (10 fl oz) Veal Stock (SEE PAGE 192)

1.   Sweat the shallot, tomato, garlic, sugar and bay leaf together in 25 g (1 oz) of the butter for 2-3 minutes, to caramelise and brown.

2.   Add the vinegar, bring to the boil, and boil to evaporate almost completely.

3.   Add the lime juice and reduce until virtually evaporated, then add the port and Noilly Prat and do the same.

4.   Add the chicken and veal stocks, bring to the boil, and simmer for 10 minutes to reduce just a little.

5.   Cut the remaining butter, which should be hard, into small pieces and melt into the sauce.

VELOUTÉ FOR FISH

This basic cream sauce for fish is best made on the day, although the reduction could be prepared in advance and frozen. Velouté is a mother sauce of several variations, see opposite.

4 PORTIONS

6 shallots, peeled and thinly sliced
15 g (½ oz) unsalted butter   500 ml (17 fl oz) white wine
500 ml (17 fl oz) Noilly Prat   1 litre (1¾ pints) double cream
1 litre (1¾ pints) Fish Stock (SEE PAGE 192)

1.   Cook the shallots in the butter until softened, without colouring.

2.   Deglaze with the white wine and Noilly Prat, and boil to reduce to a syrup.

3.   Add the fish stock and reduce by half.

4.   Add the cream, bring to the boil and simmer for 5 minutes to reduce to a coating consistency.

5.   Pass through a fine sieve. Chill covered with cling film if not using immediately.

This velouté variation is good with the cod dish on page 81.

SABAYON OF GRAIN MUSTARD

4 PORTIONS

400 ml (14 fl oz) Velouté for Fish (see left)
4 egg yolks
4 tablespoons warm clarified butter
4 tablespoons double cream, whipped
2 teaspoons grain mustard

1. Gently beat the egg yolks with a few drops of water in a round-bottomed bowl over a bain-marie. As the egg yolks thicken and cook smoothly, add the warm clarified butter and remove from the heat.

2. Separately reduce the velouté by half and allow to cool slightly
3. Add the smooth thickened egg mixture to this with the whipped cream and the mustard. The texture should be thick but still pourable

SAUCE TAPENADE

Per 50-85 ml (2-3 fl oz) individual portion of Velouté for Fish (see left) add and mix in 1 tablespoon Tapenade (SEE PAGE 206). Finish with

15 g (½ oz) unsalted butter, cut into dice. This is good with salmon confit (SEE PAGE 88).

Yet another good fish sauce, ideal with salmon, turbot, John Dory, red mullet and sea bass. The reduction could be prepared in advance and frozen. Add the cream later.

SAUCE LIE DE VIN

4 PORTIONS

2 shallots, peeled and finely sliced
160 g (5¾ oz) unsalted butter
650 ml (22 fl oz) red wine
85 ml (3 fl oz) ruby port
250 ml (9 fl oz) Fish Stock (SEE PAGE 192)
250 ml (9 fl oz) Veal Stock (SEE PAGE 192)
½ star anise   50 ml (2 fl oz) double cream
salt and freshly ground white pepper

1. Sweat the shallot in 15 g (½ oz) of the butter until softened, without colouring.
2. Add the wine and port, and boil to reduce by two-thirds.
3. In another pan boil the fish and veal stocks together with the star anise to reduce by half.

4. Add the stock reduction to the wine and port reduction. Boil together for 5 minutes, then pass through a muslin cloth into yet another pan.
5. Add the cream, and return to the stove. Dice the remaining butter and whisk into the sauce. Season to taste.

199

WHITE WINE CREAM SAUCE

This is served with fish.

4 PORTIONS

2 shallots, peeled and chopped
½ bay leaf   1 small sprig thyme
25 g (1 oz) unsalted butter   400 ml (14 fl oz) white wine
400 ml (14 fl oz) Fish Stock (SEE PAGE 192)
400 ml (14 fl oz) double cream

1. Sweat the shallot, bay leaf and thyme in the butter to soften, without colouring.
2. Add the white wine and boil to reduce down until there is about 100 ml (3½ fl oz) left.
3. Add the fish stock and do the same, boiling to reduce to 100 ml (3½ fl oz). Half-way through this reduction, change pans, for the colour of the reduction may change due to deposits on the sides of the pan.
4. Add the double cream and bring to the boil. Cook for 3-4 minutes, then pass through muslin or a fine sieve.

SAUTERNES SAUCE

This is a good sauce to serve with fish.

4 PORTIONS

4 shallots, peeled and very finely sliced
4 button mushrooms, very finely sliced
100 g (4 oz) unsalted butter
185 ml (6½ fl oz) Sauternes (sweet white wine)
100 ml (3½ fl oz) Double Chicken Stock (SEE PAGE 191)
100 ml (3½ fl oz) Fish Stock (SEE PAGE 192)
150 ml (5 fl oz) double cream   salt and freshly ground white pepper

1. Sweat the shallot and mushroom in 15 g (½ oz) of the butter until softened. Do not colour.
2. Add the Sauternes and boil to reduce by half. Do the same with the chicken stock, and then the fish stock.
3. Add the double cream and simmer for 2 minutes, then pass through a fine sieve into a clean pan. Return to the stove.
4. Dice the remaining butter and whisk into the sauce over gentle heat. Season to taste.

SAUCE NERO

This black sauce is served with seafood.

4 PORTIONS

2 shallots, peeled and sliced
25 g (1 oz) unsalted butter   200 ml (7 fl oz) white wine
200 ml (7 fl oz) Fish Stock (SEE PAGE 192)
200 ml (7 fl oz) double cream
salt and freshly ground white pepper   50 ml (2 fl oz) squid ink

1. Sweat the shallot in the butter without colouring until soft.
2. Add the wine and boil to reduce by half.
3. Add the stock and again reduce by half.
4. Add the cream and cook for 5 more minutes.
5. Season to taste, then add the squid ink to create a velvet black sauce. Sieve.

We serve this sauce with the zander dish on page 85.

4 PORTIONS

10 juniper berries
150 g (5 oz) unsalted butter
1 shallot, peeled and chopped
100 ml (3½ fl oz) white wine
100 ml (3½ fl oz) Fish Stock (SEE PAGE 192)
1 tablespoon double cream
salt and freshly ground white pepper

JUNIPER BERRY
BUTTER SAUCE

1. Crush the juniper berries lightly.
2. Heat 25 g (1 oz) of the butter in a small pan, add the berries and shallot, and sweat without colouring.
3. Pour in the wine and boil to reduce by three-quarters of its original volume. Add the fish stock and reduce similarly.
4. Add the cream, bring to the boil, and whisk in the rest of the butter. Pass the sauce through a chinois sieve. Season to taste with salt and pepper.

This is a good sauce for fish, particularly the Ravioli of Langoustines on page 29.

8 PORTIONS

¼ medium pineapple   50 g (2 oz) unsalted butter
100 g (4 oz) caster sugar
200 ml (7 fl oz) sherry vinegar   500 ml (17 fl oz) water
150 g (5 oz) tomato ketchup   500 ml (17 fl oz) double cream

**SWEET AND SOUR
PINEAPPLE CREAM**

1. Remove the skin from the pineapple and cut the flesh into small cubes.
2. Melt the butter in a frying pan and fry the pineapple cubes until they start to colour.
3. Add the sugar and keep stirring until the sugar starts to caramelise, then add the sherry vinegar and reduce to almost nothing.
4. Add the water then the tomato ketchup, and bring to the boil. Add the double cream and simmer for about 8-10 minutes.
5. Liquidise the sauce, and pass through a fine chinois sieve.

The basis for this butter sauce for fish can be made at least a week in advance, and then the butter added at more or less the last moment, about an hour in advance if kept in a warm place.

4-6 PORTIONS

juice and finely grated zest of 1 pink grapefruit, 1 orange,
2 lemons and 1 lime
200 ml (7 fl oz) white wine vinegar
100 g (3½ fl oz) champagne vinegar
1 stalk lemongrass   3 cloves   2 sprigs lemon balm
60 ml (2¼ fl oz) double cream
60 g (2¼ oz) hard unsalted butter, diced

**CITRUS BUTTER
SAUCE**

1.   Bring the citrus juices and zest, vinegars, spices and herbs to the boil in a suitable pan. Cook for 10 minutes, then leave to cool. Chill for at least 1 week for the flavours to blend.

2.   Reduce the fragrant liquid down to about 200 ml (7 fl oz). Strain.
3.   Add the cream, melt in the butter, and serve.

SAUCE HOLLANDAISE

This mother sauce is the basis for béarnaise sauce and paloise sauce, both wonderful accompaniments to meat.

4 PORTIONS

100 ml (3½ fl oz) white wine vinegar
10 white peppercorns, lightly crushed
a few parsley stalks   1 shallot, peeled and chopped
50 ml (2 fl oz) water   1 tablespoon white wine
2 egg yolks   juice of ½ lemon
salt and cayenne pepper
250 g (9 oz) clarified butter, at blood temperature

1.   Put the vinegar, peppercorns, parsley stalks and shallot into a suitable pan and boil to reduce by about half.
2.   Leave for 24 hours to infuse, then add the water and wine and strain.
3.   Place the egg yolks in a bowl with the lemon juice, and salt and cayenne to taste. Whisk together, then gradually whisk in the strained vinegar reduction until you have a nice sabayon. The liquid must be added slowly; as it deflates the egg yolks, it strengthens them.

4.   After 10 minutes or so of whipping, put the bowl over a bain-marie, and add the butter gradually. Whip until all the butter has been added and you have a good emulsion. The sauce should be thick and to the ribbon (when the lifted whisk leaves a ribbon-like trail on the surface of the sauce). The sauce can now stand for up to 2 hours if kept in the bowl in a bain-marie, with the water not exceeding 50°C/122°F.

SAUCE BÉARNAISE

This is served with steak (SEE PAGE 136).

Add several stalks of tarragon to the Hollandaise vinegar and other ingredients before boiling, reducing and infusing. Make the sauce as above, but add about 25 very finely chopped tarragon leaves to the sauce just as you serve, *not before.*

SAUCE PALOISE

This is served with roast rump of lamb (SEE PAGE 132).

Add several fresh mint stalks to the Hollandaise vinegar and other ingredients before boiling, reducing and infusing. Make the sauce as above, but add about 25 very finely chopped mint leaves to the sauce just as you serve, *not before.*

This light summery sauce is served with grilled salmon

SAUCE MOUSSELINE

Into each 600 ml (1 pint) of basic Sauce Hollandaise, whisk 300 ml (10 fl oz) semi-whipped double cream.

This is good infused with herbs, as a sauce for meats (the rabbit on page 125, for instance).

DOUBLE CHICKEN BUTTER

4 PORTIONS

100 ml (3½ fl oz) Double Chicken Stock *(SEE PAGE 191)*
1 dessertspoon double cream
100 g (4 oz) hard unsalted butter, diced
1 sprig herb of choice (optional)

1. Bring the stock to the boil.
2. Whisk in the cream, followed by the butter dice.

3. If using a herb, infuse it in the hot butter for 10 minutes, then pass the sauce through a chinois sieve.

This sauce is good with fish, and has a few variations.

BEURRE BLANC

4 PORTIONS

1 teaspoon white wine vinegar   2 teaspoons white wine
2 shallots, peeled and very finely chopped
1 teaspoon double cream
250 g (9 oz) hard unsalted butter, diced
salt and freshly ground white pepper

1. Place the vinegar, wine and shallot in a small pan and reduce to a syrup.
2. Add the cream and reduce a little more.

3. Add the butter dice and whisk in until amalgamated. Stir in seasonings to taste, then pass through a fine sieve.

This is good with the smoked haddock on page 82.

MUSTARD BEURRE BLANC

Stir 1 tablespoon grain mustard into the basic beurre blanc after sieving it.

SAUCE NANTAISE

Sweat 2 chopped shallots in 15 g (½ oz) unsalted butter to soften, then add 25 ml (1 fl oz) white wine vinegar. Reduce until almost evapo-

This is good with the skate dish on page 69.

rated, then stir into the basic beurre blanc after sieving it.

MAYONNAISE

A classic recipe with a hint of white heat.

4-6 PORTIONS

2 egg yolks
1 tablespoon Dijon mustard
2 tablespoons white wine vinegar
1 teaspoon salt
a dash of Tabasco
500 ml (17 fl oz) peanut oil

1. Place the egg yolks, mustard, vinegar, salt and Tabasco in a bowl and mix together until the salt has dissolved.
2. Add the oil in drops at first, whisking in so that the yolks can absorb the oil.
3. When about half the oil has been added,

it can be added in slightly larger amounts, but continue whisking.
4. Whisk well until all the oil has been added, and the sauce has become thick and creamy. Store it in the fridge, covered, for up to a week.

TOMATO SAUCE

This is a rich tasting tomato sauce, ideal with the cabbage 'balls' on page 54, and the monkfish and bean dish on page 67.

4 PORTIONS

40 g (1½ oz) diced carrot
40 g (1½ oz) diced onion
2 garlic cloves, peeled and crushed
25 ml (1 fl oz) goose fat
40 g (1½ oz) plain flour
10 g (¼ oz) Parma ham, chopped
400 g (14 oz) plum tomatoes, skinned and seeded and chopped
salt and freshly ground white pepper
50 g (2 oz) unsalted butter (optional)

1. Soften the carrot, onion and garlic in the goose fat for a few minutes without colouring, then stir in the flour and cook gently for 15-20 minutes.
2. Add the ham and tomatoes to the pan, and bring the mixture to the boil. Add salt and

pepper to taste, and cook steadily for 30 minutes, covered.
3. Blend the sauce in a liquidiser, then push through a fine sieve. Don't reboil it, but heat gently, and add the butter if required, to give the sauce a gloss.

This tomato sauce is ideal with the crab and avocado tian on page 23, but it also goes well with most cold starters, a tuna salad, and even some warm fish dishes.

page 23

4 PORTIONS

25 ml (1 fl oz) red wine vinegar
15 g (½ oz) tomato purée   10 g (¼ oz) tomato ketchup
250 g (9 oz) tomato pulp
25 ml (1 fl oz) olive oil
a dash of Tabasco
salt and freshly ground white pepper

SAUCE GAZPACHO

1. Liquidise the red wine vinegar, tomato purée, tomato ketchup and tomato pulp together, then pass through a chinois sieve.

2. Add the olive oil, dash of Tabasco, and seasoning to taste, and mix together well.

This is a wonderful fresh sauce, best served with fish and shellfish.

4 PORTIONS

85 ml (3 fl oz) olive oil   25 ml (1 fl oz) lemon juice
1 teaspoon coriander seeds, crushed
8 basil leaves, cut into julienne strips
2 tomatoes, skinned, seeded and diced

SAUCE VIERGE

1. Heat the oil gently in a small pan, then add the lemon juice. Remove from the heat.
2. Add the coriander and basil, and leave to infuse in the warm oil for a few minutes.

3. Add the tomato dice and serve immediately.

This cold sauce, good with the terrine on page 52, will last a couple of days in the fridge.

page 52

4 PORTIONS

2 hard-boiled eggs, shelled
the same weight each of capers and small gherkins (cornichons)
½ tablespoon chopped tarragon
1½ tablespoons chopped parsley
2-2½ tablespoons olive oil

SAUCE GRIBICHE

1. Weigh the eggs out of their shells, and then measure out the same weight of both capers and gherkins.
2. Separate the yolks from the whites; sieve the yolks and finely chop the whites. Chop the capers and gherkins. Mix all together in a bowl.

3. Add the fresh chopped herbs to the bowl, and then pour in about 2 tablespoons of the oil gradually, mixing just to bind. You may need a little more oil, but the texture should be of a nice paste, not runny.

VINAIGRETTE

This keeps well for up to a week.

MAKES 400 ML (14 FL OZ)

75 ml (2¾ fl oz) white wine vinegar
salt and freshly ground white pepper
120 ml (4 fl oz) peanut oil
200 ml (7 fl oz) olive oil

1. Place the vinegar in a bowl and add a pinch each of salt and pepper. Stir with a whisk to dissolve.

2. Add the oils and whisk to an emulsion. Taste and adjust seasoning if necessary. Store in a suitable container.

TOMATO FONDUE

This is like a fresh tomato sauce, which is useful in a number of recipes, especially fish. It could be made a couple of days in advance.

MAKES ABOUT 150 ML (5 FL OZ)

6-8 large ripe plum tomatoes, skinned, seeded and diced
100 ml (3½ fl oz) olive oil
½ shallot, peeled and finely chopped
1 garlic clove, peeled and finely chopped
1 sprig thyme
¼ bay leaf

1. Heat the olive oil in a pan and sweat the shallot and garlic for a few minutes without colouring.
2. Add the tomato dice, thyme and bay. Cook very gently over a low heat until all the

moisture has been removed from the tomato, and you are left with a dry tomato paste, which is full of flavour.
3. Remove the herbs, and put the mixture in the blender. Blend until smooth.

TAPENADE

We use this in a fish sauce, and as a fish garnish, but it is also good on warm toast as a canapé.

8 PORTIONS

250 g (9 oz) good black olives, stoned
50 g (2 oz) anchovies
25 g (1 oz) capers, drained
1½ garlic cloves, peeled
2 tablespoons olive oil

1. Place all the ingredients, apart from the olive oil, into a blender. Blend for about 5 minutes, then add the oil.

2. Decant into small clean jars with screw-on lids, and store in the fridge. It will keep for up to 3 months.

A good garnish for meat. Make in the morning, if you like, and heat up gently to serve.

4 PORTIONS

*8-12 large shallots or button onions
rock salt
2 bay leaves   1 sprig thyme
300 ml (10 fl oz) olive oil*

1.   Trim the root of the shallots or onions, and take off any loose leaves of skin, leaving a perfect shape, still with the skin on.
2.   Cover the bottom of a small ovenproof pan with rock salt. Place the shallots or onions on top of the salt and add the bay leaves, thyme and the olive oil.
3.   Cover with foil and cook for 3 hours in the oven preheated to 150°C/300°F/Gas 2, or until the shallots are tender.

These garlic cloves make a good garnish for a number of dishes, both fish and meat. Make in advance, a day at most. You could confit shallots in much the same way.

4 PORTIONS

*12-16 large garlic cloves, unpeeled
goose fat to cover
2 bay leaves   2 small sprigs thyme*

1.   Half fill a small saucepan with the goose fat, and then place on the stove until the temperature reaches about 90°C/194°F.
2.   Add the bay leaves, thyme and garlic. Bring the fat back to about 80°C/176°F. Cook at this temperature for about 20-30 minutes.
3.   After 20 minutes, check to see if the garlic is tender to the touch. if it is, remove from the heat and allow to cool in the fat.
4.   Store in the goose fat in the fridge. To serve, remove from the fat, and fry in a dry pan to crisp up.

Good with liver and plain poultry and meat.

4 PORTIONS

*4 large potatoes
salt and freshly ground white pepper
25 ml (1 fl oz) vegetable oil
1 garlic clove, peeled and crushed
50 g (2 oz) Brioche crumbs (SEE PAGE 217)
25 g (1 oz) parsley, finely chopped*

1.   Peel and wash the potatoes, then dice into 1 cm (½ in) squares.
2.   Blanch the potato dice in boiling salted water for a few minutes, then drain them, and dry them well.
3.   Sauté the potato dice in the hot oil until golden brown, about 5-6 minutes.
4.   Add the crushed garlic, brioche crumbs and parsley, and toss until the potatoes are covered. Serve immediately.

POMME ANNA

This potato cake, made in a small ovenproof pan, and served in wedges, is good with poultry, lamb and steak.

6 PORTIONS

5 medium potatoes
salt and freshly ground white pepper
100 g (4 oz) clarified unsalted butter
25 ml (1 fl oz) goose fat

1. Preheat the oven to 180°C/350°F/Gas 4, and have ready a heavy-bottomed, non-stick ovenproof pan about 14-15 cm (5½-6 in) in diameter.
2. Peel and slice the potatoes very thinly. Season with salt and leave in a colander for a while.
3. Squeeze the potato slices gently, so that all the liquid is removed, but do not wash: you want to retain the starch.
4. Take 10 nice slices and arrange them, overlapping, around the base of the pan, starting in the middle. This will be the top of your potato cake, so work neatly.
5. Put in 25 g (1 oz) of the clarified butter and cook until the slices become crisp and golden brown. Do not let them stick, though. Remove from the heat.

6. Add the remaining clarified butter and the goose fat to the remaining potato slices, mix to coat, and then arrange the slices neatly on top of the crisp layer in the pan, building up to a tower that comes about 1 cm (½ in) over the top of the pan.
7. Put a butter paper on top, place in the pre-heated oven, and cook for 45-60 minutes. About four or five times during the cooking, remove from the oven and press the 'tower' down.
8. Test with a skewer to ensure that the potato is tender, then press down hard in the pan. Drain off any surplus fat. Put a plate over the top of the pan, and turn over so that the potato cake slips out on to the plate, the crisp initial slices to the top.
9. Slice into wedges to serve.

POMME FONDANT

Good with poultry, lamb and steak. You could make about an hour in advance, which allows the potato to absorb the butter. Cut the potatoes into different shapes — into 'banana' shapes, or, thickly, into circles.

4 PORTIONS

4 medium potatoes
100 g (4 oz) unsalted butter, diced
salt and freshly ground white pepper
50 ml (2 fl oz) water

1. Peel and square off each potato. Using a 5 cm (2 in) plain round cutter, cut a fondant shape out of each potato square. Using a potato peeler, round off the sharp edges of each fondant. It should look like a large olive.
2. Using a saucepan with a base diameter of about 15 cm (6 in), so that the fondants can sit comfortably in the bottom, line the bottom of the pan with the diced butter.
3. Place the fondant potatoes on to the butter and season with salt and pepper. Pour the water on to this, and cook on a slow heat for about 15 minutes on either side until the potatoes are golden brown.

Try to use a potato such as Désirée that will crisp up well. Good with any meat, and makes a base for a fillet steak.

POMME RÖSTI

4 PORTIONS

*2 large Désirée potatoes
salt
50 g (2 oz) clarified butter*

1. Peel the potatoes, slice them finely, then cut into julienne strips, neither too thick nor too thin.
2. Salt the strips and leave hanging in a cloth for the liquid to drip out. Squeeze to get the potato strips as dry as possible.
3. Mix the dried potato with the warm clarified butter.
4. There are several ways of proceeding now. If you have an electric or solid fuel hob, divide the potato between four Tefal galette moulds of 7.5 cm (3 in) in diameter. Press down evenly and then place the bottom of the mould over the heat. The heat must not be too high, or the base of the rösti will burn and the inside will not be cooked, or too low. Cook for 5-7 minutes altogether.
5. Or, on other hobs, use a non-stick frying pan with similar sized round cutters. Push the potato into them, smooth and then fry first one side, then, pushing down again, the other.
   You could of course, just cook in tablespoonfuls, but you really want that nice even shape.

Good with fish.

POMME SAUTÉ

4 PORTIONS

*4 large baking potatoes
salt
goose fat*

1. Wash the potatoes well, then cook in boiling salted water until two-thirds done. Remove the potatoes from the water and allow to cool before skinning.
2. Cut each potato into five slices, then use a round cutter to make them uniform.
3. Fry them in goose fat until golden brown. Drain well, and serve as soon as you can.

This could be made a day or so in advance. It's good with pigeon, quail, duck and ham.

BRAISED CABBAGE

4 PORTIONS

*1 whole white cabbage
50 ml (2 fl oz) goose fat
1 garlic clove, peeled and finely chopped
½ large shallot, peeled and finely chopped
100 g (4 oz) smoked bacon, rinded and cut into fine strips (lardons)
200 ml (7 fl oz) Veal Stock (SEE PAGE 192)
100 ml (3½ fl oz) Chicken Stock (SEE PAGE 190)*

1. Preheat the oven to 160°C/325°F/Gas 3.
2. Cut the cabbage into four. Remove and discard the coarse stalk, then shred the leaves finely.
3. Heat the goose fat and fry off the garlic and shallot until softened, then add the *lardons* and cook until golden brown.

4. Add the cabbage, sweating it off and making sure that most of the natural water in the cabbage has evaporated.
5. Add the veal and chicken stocks and bring to the boil. Cover with a lid and cook in the preheated oven for 30 minutes, or until tender.

BRAISED LETTUCE

Braised lettuce is delicious served with calf's liver; see pages 143 and 144.

4 PORTIONS

*4 small Cos or Baby Gem lettuces
salt and freshly ground white pepper
1 carrot, peeled and finely diced
1 small celeriac, peeled and finely diced
1 small onion, peeled and finely diced
1 celery stalk, finely diced   25 g (1 oz) unsalted butter
350 ml (12 fl oz) Veal Stock (SEE PAGE 192)
1 bay leaf   1 sprig thyme*

1. Remove and discard the outer leaves of the lettuces if necessary. Halve the lettuces, and blanch quickly in boiling salted water. Refresh in cold water, then drain well.
2. Sweat the vegetable dice in the butter in a braising dish until they have some colour.

3. Place the lettuce pieces on top of the diced vegetables, and add the stock, herbs and some salt and pepper.
4. Bring to the boil, then cover and braise until tender, about 10-15 minutes, depending on size.

ARTICHOKES BARIGOULE

These make a delicious starter by themselves, but we use them as a base for fish.

10 PORTIONS

*10 medium artichokes, base and leaves trimmed
3 medium carrots, peeled and thinly sliced
2 small onions, peeled and thinly sliced
6 garlic cloves, peeled and crushed
1 large sprig fennel herb
250 ml (8 fl oz) good olive oil   250 ml (8 fl oz) white wine
250 ml (8 fl oz) Chicken Stock (SEE PAGE 190)
salt and freshly ground white pepper
1 bunch basil*

1. Sweat the artichokes, carrot, onion, half the crushed garlic and the fennel in the olive oil for a few minutes until softened and browned.
2. Add the wine and stock, and some salt and pepper. Mince enough basil leaves to make 1 tablespoon, and add to the liquid.

3. Bring to the boil, cover and simmer until the artichokes are cooked, about 15-20 minutes, depending on size.
4. Mince another tablespoon's worth of basil leaves, and add to the artichokes, along with the remaining crushed garlic.

A good garnish for tuna, see page 100, but it can also be used as an accompaniment: double the recipe. It can serve as a 'pâté' as well.

see page 100

AUBERGINE CAVIAR

AT LEAST 4 GARNISH PORTIONS

*1 medium aubergine
1 garlic clove, peeled and sliced
1 sprig thyme   1 sprig rosemary   1 bay leaf
100 ml (3½ fl oz) olive oil
salt and freshly ground white pepper
1 medium tomato, skinned, seeded and finely diced*

1.   Preheat the oven to 140°C/275°F/Gas 1, and have ready a piece of kitchen foil, 60 cm (2 feet) square.
2.   Cut the aubergine in half lengthways and make criss-cross cuts into the flesh with a sharp knife. Do not cut through to the skin. Into these cuts insert slivers of garlic, the thyme and rosemary leaves, and little pieces of the bay leaf. Pour over the olive oil and season.
3.   Wrap loosely but securely in the doubled foil, and bake in the preheated slow oven for 1 hour.
4.   Remove the aubergine from the oven and the foil, and scrape the flesh from the skin on to the work surface. Chop very finely with a sharp knife.
5.   Add the tomato dice to the aubergine flesh as and when needed. Season if required.

Serve with fish. It should be made about 4 hours in advance, but can be stored in the fridge for a day or so.

AUBERGINE CONFIT

4 PORTIONS

*2 medium aubergines
1 medium onion, peeled and finely chopped
200 ml (7 fl oz) olive oil
2 beef tomatoes, sliced
25 ml (1 fl oz) balsamic vinegar
25 ml (1 fl oz) sherry vinegar
½ teaspoon thyme leaves
50 g (2 oz) honey   1 garlic clove, peeled and crushed
5 g (¼ oz) white peppercorns, coarsely crushed
5 g (¼ oz) coriander seeds, coarsely crushed*

1.   Sweat the onion in about 1 tablespoon of olive oil until softened, then add the sliced tomato.
2.   Turn up the heat, and deglaze the pan with the vinegars. Bring to the boil.
3.   Add the thyme leaves, honey, garlic, peppercorns and coriander seeds, and then remove the pan from the heat.
4.   Cut the aubergine into 2 cm (¾ in) thick slices, and fry these in the remaining oil, using the oil gradually. Fry to colour the slices, but not to cook them.
5.   Mix the tomato mixture and the aubergine slices in a shallow heatproof container, cover with foil, and cook gently on top of the stove for about 1 hour.
6.   Cool and store in a sealed container in the fridge.

211

COUSCOUS

This can be served cold as a salad, but we use it as a garnish for the pan-fried mullet fillets on page 94.

4 PORTIONS

300 g (11 oz) quick couscous
150 ml (5 fl oz) Chicken Stock (SEE PAGE 190)
1 red pepper, seeded and diced
¼ cucumber, diced   4 shallots, peeled and diced
100 ml (3½ fl oz) olive oil   juice of 2 lemons
salt and freshly ground white pepper
1 teaspoon each of chopped mint and coriander

1. Place the couscous in a bowl and pour over the boiling chicken stock. Mix so that the couscous is moistened and swells.

2. Mix in the pepper, cucumber and shallot dice, olive oil and lemon juice, and season with salt and pepper. Mix in the herbs.

LENTILLES DU PAYS

This earthy lentil dish is served with roast breast of duck at The Canteen, but it is good with several meats.

4 PORTIONS

225 g (8 oz) Puy lentils
1 sprig thyme   ½ bay leaf   1 garlic clove, peeled
1 litre (1¾ pints) Chicken Stock (SEE PAGE 190)
15 g (½ oz) unsalted butter
25 g (1 oz) smoked bacon, diced
25 g (1 oz) each of carrot, celery and shallot, diced
salt and freshly ground white pepper

1. Soak the lentils in water for 8 hours.
2. Drain the lentils, and place in a pan with the thyme, bay, garlic and enough stock to cover. Bring to the boil and then simmer for 10 minutes. Drain the lentils, remove the herbs and garlic, and leave to cool.

3. When you wish to serve, heat the butter in a large frying pan over a moderate heat, and add the bacon and vegetable dice. Sweat gently until soft.
4. Add the lentils and cook gently to warm them through. Season to taste.

RATATOUILLE

This is a drier than normal ratatouille which is very useful as a garnish. Double the recipe if using as an accompaniment.

4 SMALL PORTIONS

2 red and 2 yellow peppers
2 large courgettes   1 small aubergine
1 small onion   1 plum tomato   olive oil
25 g (1 oz) fresh Tomato Fondue (SEE PAGE 206)
6 fresh basil leaves, cut into thin strips
salt and freshly ground white pepper

1. Skin and seed the peppers, then cut them into small dice. Cut the skin and a little flesh from the courgettes and aubergine - about 5 mm (¼ in) thick - and then dice this (use the remaining flesh in another dish). Peel and cut the onion into small dice. Skin, seed and dice the tomato.
2. Heat a little olive oil in a large pan and cook the pepper dice gently for a few minutes. They should still be crisp and bright in colour.

Remove with a slotted spoon to a plate.
3. Do the same with the courgette, aubergine and onion dice, cooking them separately in a little olive oil
4. Heat the tomato fondue gently in a thick-based pan, add the basil and cook for 1 minute.
5. Add all the vegetable dice to this, and gently mix together over gentle heat. Season.

These 'stuffed' leaves make a good garnish for red mullet and any grilled fish. They could also be served as a canapé. The batter can be used to coat deep-fried salsify, green beans or other vegetables. Fry the beignets at the last moment.

BEIGNETS OF SAGE

4 PORTIONS

at least 16 large fresh sage leaves
1 tablespoon Tapenade (SEE PAGE 206)
olive oil for shallow-frying

BATTER

25 g (1 oz) fresh yeast
250 ml (8 fl oz) beer or lager
200 g (7 oz) plain flour, sieved
a pinch of salt

1. For the batter, dissolve the yeast in a little of the beer which has been warmed gently on the stove to blood temperature. Then incorporate the rest of the beer.
2. Place the flour in a bowl and make a well in the centre. Slowly pour in the beer and yeast mixture, whisking continuously until all has been

incorporated. The batter should be quite runny. Stand for about 3 hours to allow it to activate.
3. Sandwich 2 sage leaves together with a little of the tapenade. Make 8 'sandwiches'.
4. Heat the olive oil in a pan. Dip the sage leaves in the batter and then shallow-fry in the hot oil until light and crisp.

This is the final finishing touch to a risotto of sea scallops; it uses the scallop roes, and adds a flavourful smoothness to the rice. It can be made up to a week in advance, and refrigerated, or it can be frozen.

ACID BUTTER

30 g (1½ oz) finely chopped onion
100 ml (3½ fl oz) white wine
50 ml (1¾ fl oz) white wine vinegar
8 scallop roes   200 g (7 oz) unsalted butter, in pieces

1. Bring the onion, wine and vinegar to the boil in a suitable pan, and boil to reduce by half.
2. Add the roes and let them cook briefly, then whisk in the butter.

3. Transfer to a food processor and purée - the mixture will turn pink.
4. Push through a sieve and then chill or freeze.

SOFT HERB CRUST

This makes a good topping for fish such as sea bass and cod. Use white breadcrumbs, preferably brioche. To make a thyme crust (for the cod on page 81), double the quantity of thyme.

4 PORTIONS

80 g (3 oz) fresh breadcrumbs
40 g (1½ oz) Gruyère cheese, grated
25 g (1 oz) parsley, chopped   ½ teaspoon chopped thyme
60 g (2½ oz) unsalted butter, softened
salt and freshly ground white pepper

1.   Place all the ingredients into a food processor and process until thoroughly mixed. Use straightaway, or freeze.

2.   To freeze, spread out on to a greaseproof-paper lined tray and open-freeze. Package in quantities suitable for later use, and re-freeze.

FROMAGE BLANC WITH HERBS

We use this as a garnish for the salmon dish on page 40, but it's actually delicious used as a sandwich filling!

250 g (9 oz) fromage blanc
50 g (2 oz) shallots, peeled and very finely chopped
15 g (½ oz) garlic, peeled and very finely chopped
a handful of chives, finely snipped
a handful of parsley, very finely chopped
250 ml (8 fl oz) double cream, whipped to soft peaks

1.   Place the fromage blanc in a piece of muslin, tie securely with string, and suspend over a bowl for 24 hours, so that every drop of liquid drips out.

2.   Fold the shallot, garlic and herbs into the fromage blanc.
3.   Fold in the double cream, and refrigerate until required.

CHICKEN MOUSSE

This is a stuffing or farce constituent, helping to bind other ingredients in the rabbit and ravioli recipes on pages 125 and 28.

4 PORTIONS

100 g (4 oz) chicken breast
salt and freshly ground white pepper
a pinch of ground mace
½ egg white   150 ml (5 fl oz) double cream

1.   Skin the chicken breast, and cut the flesh into small pieces.
2.   Place in the food processor, season with salt, pepper and mace, and process to a purée.

3.   Cool a little before briefly blending in the egg white and cream.
4.   Push through a fine sieve, then chill if not using immediately.

Make in advance and use as a garnish for fish dishs, see pages 75 and 81.

MAKES ABOUT 50 G (2 OZ)

225 g (8 oz) cultivated mushrooms
salt and freshly ground white pepper
1 tablespoon double cream

1. Wipe the mushrooms and trim the stalks if necessary. Chop both caps and stalks very finely in a processor; or you can do it by hand, using a sharp knife.

2. Heat in a dry pan until their liquid comes out and evaporates, and the mushrooms shrink.
3. Season to taste. Add the cream and mix in to bind the mushrooms.

This can be made in advance and frozen.

MAKES 600 G (1¼ LB)

600 g (1¼ lb) plain white flour
4 eggs   6 egg yolks
2 tablespoons olive oil   a pinch of salt

1. Place the flour in a food processor, and switch the machine on.
2. Slowly add the eggs and egg yolks, using the pulse button.
3. When all the egg has been amalgamated, add the olive oil and salt and mix in briefly.
4. Remove from the machine and knead for a few minutes on a lightly floured surface until even and smooth. Divide into 8 equal-sized pieces, cover with cling film, and allow to rest for at least an hour before rolling and cutting as appropriate. Any pasta not to be used straightaway can now be frozen.

5. If using a pasta machine, it is easy to roll out to a paper thin-ness, and cut into noodles, lasagne sheets etc. Otherwise work by hand, and use a rolling pin to roll the dough paper thin. Cut into noodles, rectangles for lasagne, or circles and other shapes for ravioli.
6. To cook noodles or lasagne, drop into boiling salted water for 30 seconds. Refresh in cold water and drain. Add a few drops of olive oil and set aside. (For ravioli cooking, see individual recipes.)
7. To serve, heat through in an emulsion of butter and water.

This pastry will keep for a day or two in the fridge, and it also freezes well. It is mainly used for desserts, for the feuillantine on page 152, and fruit tart bases, for instance. We tend to use it baked flat, though, not risen like conventional puff pastry. It is also good used in a savoury dish, as a wrapping for skate (see page 69).

MAKES ABOUT 1.1 KG (2½ LB)

450 g (1 lb) strong plain flour, sieved
1 teaspoon salt
450 g (1 lb) unsalted butter, softened slightly
180 ml (6½ fl oz) water
2 teaspoons white wine vinegar

1. Sieve the flour into a circle on your work surface. Make a well in the middle and put into this the salt, 60 g (2¼ oz) of the butter, the water and the vinegar. Mix and knead until the dough is smooth and elastic. Mould the dough into a ball and score a cross with a knife across the top. Cover the dough with a cloth and leave to rest in a cool place for about an hour.

2. On a lightly floured surface, roll the dough into a sheet about 20 cm (8 in) square, rolling the corners (the tails of the cross) a little more thinly than the centre.

3. Place the remaining butter in a block in the centre of the dough. Bring up the four corners of pastry over the butter to make an envelope.

4. Roll this out into a rectangle about 25 x 15 (10 x 6 in) and fold in three. Turn this folded rectangle by 90 degrees. This constitutes a 'turn'.

5. Ensuring the rolling pin is at right angles to the folds, roll out again to a rectangle the same size as before, and fold in three again as before. Again turn the pastry by 90 degrees (in the same direction as before). Two 'turns' have now been completed.

6. Cover the dough and rest in the fridge for an hour.

7. Roll out again twice in a rectangle, fold and turn as in steps 4 and 5. Four 'turns' have now been completed. Rest the dough again in the fridge for another hour.

8. Repeat stages 4 and 5 again. Six 'turns' have now been completed. Rest the dough for one more hour in the fridge, and the dough is ready for use.

SWEET PASTRY

This is the pastry to use for sweet tarts (see pages 177-178). You will need roughly half this quantity – 500 g or 18 oz – per tart. It freezes well, but do wrap carefully.

MAKES 1 KG (2¼ LB)

700 g (1½ lb) unsalted butter
300 g (11 oz) icing sugar
8 egg yolks
100 ml (3½ fl oz) water   1 kg (2¼ lb) plain flour

1. Cream the butter and icing sugar together in an electric mixer bowl until soft and white.

2. Add the egg yolks and beat in thoroughly. Turn the machine off, remove the lid, and scrape the sides down into the mixture to make sure everything is incorporated. Cover with the lid and blend again.

3. Add a little of the water, then add the flour, and mix together thoroughly. Stop the machine every now and again to scrape the sides down.

4. Add the remaining water and mix for 2-3 minutes.

5. Remove, wrap in cling film and chill for at least 1 hour before using.

SWEET PASTRY TART CASE

1. Roll out 500 g (18 oz) pastry to 5 mm (¼ in) thick, and use to line a 20 cm (8 in) tart ring on a baking sheet, or a tin with a removable base. The ring should be 3.75 cm (1½ in) deep. Do not cut excess pastry off the top at this stage.

2. Rest for at least an hour in the fridge to ensure the pastry will not shrink.

3. Meanwhile, preheat the oven to 180°C/ 350°F/Gas 4.

4. Line the pastry case with greaseproof paper or foil, and fill with baking beans. Bake blind in the preheated oven for about 15 minutes.

5. Remove from the oven, remove the foil and beans, and leave to settle for a moment or two. Then bake for about 5 minutes more until nice and golden. Keep in the ring, and cool before filling and baking again (if necessary). Trim the overlapping pastry when ready to eat.

This biscuit mixture is useful in a number of ways. If made into actual biscuits, they are good by themselves, but also make a delicious base for the Tiramisu on page 156. The mixture can also be baked flat on a baking sheet when it can be used as the base for the Champagne Mousse on page 160.

BISCUIT CUILLÈRE

MAKES 16 BISCUITS

3 eggs, separated   70 g (2¾ oz) caster sugar
75 g (3 oz) plain flour, sieved   icing sugar

1.   Preheat the oven to 200°C/400°F/Gas 6, and grease a large baking tray with a little extra butter.
2.   Whisk the egg whites and sugar together until stiff, then slowly mix in the egg yolks. Fold in the flour. Mix together until smooth.

3.   Place this mixture in a piping bag and pipe on to the baking tray into 16 fingers. They should be about 6.25 cm (2½ in) long and 2.5 cm (1 in) wide.
4.   Dust the fingers with icing sugar and bake for 10 minutes in the preheated oven.

These crisp filigree bowl-shaped biscuits make wonderful containers for many desserts - the Tiramisu on page 156, for instance, and many sorbets and ice creams.

TUILES (TULIP BASKETS)

MAKES 8-10 BISCUITS

100 g (4 oz) unsalted butter
120 g (4½ oz) caster sugar
4 egg whites   100 g (4 oz) plain flour

1.   Preheat the oven to 180°C/350°F/Gas 4, and grease a large baking tray (or trays).
2.   Cream the butter and sugar together until white and creamy, then add the egg whites, one at a time.
3.   Finally fold in the flour.
4.   Spoon tablespoons of the mixture on to the tray(s) and spread out to thin circles. Do not let

them touch. You should have between 8 and 10.
5.   Cook until golden brown in the preheated oven, for about 4-5 minutes (but this depends on the oven), then remove.
6.   Quickly place each tuile over a suitable mould (a ramekin or small pudding basin bottom, for instance). Leave to cool and set over the mould. Store carefully in airtight containers.

This bread can be made in a traditional brioche à tête mould, in a terrine, or in individual loaf tins or moulds. Start it the day before you want to bake. It's good, toasted, with many starters. The dough can also be made into savoury dumplings; see overleaf.

BRIOCHE

MAKES 1 LARGE LOAF OR 10 INDIVIDUAL LOAVES

12 g (scant ½ oz) fresh yeast   1 tablespoon water
30 g (1¼ oz) caster sugar   300 g (11 oz) plain flour
6 g (scant ¼ oz) salt   3½ eggs
175 g (6 oz) softened unsalted butter

TO FINISH
1 egg, beaten

1. Mix the yeast with the water and a pinch of the sugar. Leave to dissolve.
2. Put the flour in a mixer, add the remaining sugar and the salt, then mix in the dissolved yeast and the 3½ eggs. Mix until smooth.
3. Add the soft butter in pieces, with the machine still running, and the dough will be ready when it comes away from the sides of the bowl.
4. Put the dough in a clean bowl, cover with a damp cloth or greased polythene or cling film, and chill for 12 hours.

5. Remove the dough from the bowl and knock back. Knead for a minute or so. Place in one greased mould or divide between 10 individual greased moulds. Leave to prove until the dough comes above the top of the container or containers.
6. Meanwhile preheat the oven to 190°C/375°F/Gas 5.
7. Egg wash the top of the loaf and bake in the preheated oven: the large will need 30 minutes, the individual loaves, at least 15 minutes. Cool.

BRIOCHE DUMPLINGS

Make these from the chilled dough. Divide the dough into 15 g (½ oz) pieces and roll into balls. Prove, then poach in stock (see page 108) for 3-4 minutes. Serve immediately.

CARAMEL SAUCE

This sauce is wonderful with the apple tart on page 182, with the Marquise on page 183, or just vanilla ice cream! Make a couple of days in advance if you like.

4 PORTIONS

60 g (2¼ oz) caster sugar   125 ml (4 fl oz) double cream

1. Melt the sugar gently in a heavy-based saucepan, then cook, just as gently, until you have a dark caramel.

2. Add the cream – carefully, as the hot caramel will make it boil and spit – and stir together to a sauce consistency.

SWEET SABAYON

This delicious sauce must be made just before serving. Choose an alcohol to complement the dish the sauce is to accompany – Calvados for an apple dish, Kirsch for a cherry or other red fruit dish.

4 PORTIONS

2 egg yolks
200 ml (7 fl oz) syrup (made from 100 g/3½ oz caster sugar and 100 ml/3½ fl oz water)
100 ml (3½ fl oz) alcohol of choice

1. Place the egg yolks, syrup and alcohol in a wide, shallow pan and whisk together.
2. Over a very gentle heat, continue to whisk until a foam starts to form.

3. Continue cooking very gently, whisking all the time, for at least 15 minutes, until the sabayon is cooked, light and fluffy. (An electric hand whisk is less exhausting.)

218

This is used as the base for the mousse on page 159, but it could also fill a tart or tartlet case. Make a day in advance.

10-15 PORTIONS

*6 egg yolks
75 g (3 oz) caster sugar   50 g (2 oz) plain flour
400 ml (14 fl oz) milk*

1.   In a pan, cream the egg yolks and sugar together well, then mix in the flour.
2.   Bring the milk to the boil in another pan then whisk a little into the egg yolk pan.

3.   Add the remainder of the liquid and cook over a gentle heat, stirring, to a smooth cream, for no longer than 5 minutes.

This basic sweet sauce is served with a variety of desserts, from Oeufs à la Neige to Bread and Butter Pudding (see pages 188 and 173).

ABOUT 10 PORTIONS

*6 egg yolks
120 g (4½ oz) caster sugar   500 ml (17 fl oz) milk
1 vanilla pod (optional)*

CRÈME ANGLAISE

1.   Mix the egg yolks and sugar together in a bowl, and bring the milk and vanilla to the boil in a pan.
2.   Pour the hot milk into the egg yolks in the bowl, mix well and swiftly, then return to the milk pan.

3.   Cook very slowly over a gentle heat, stirring constantly, until the mixture thickens enough to coat the back of your spoon.
4.   Remove from the heat and pass through a fine sieve into a jug, or bowl or bowls. Leave to cool. Cover the surface with cling film.

COFFEE CRÈME ANGLAISE
Add 20 g (¾ oz) instant coffee powder, diluted in a little water, to the basic crème anglaise.

LIQUEUR CRÈME ANGLAISE
Add a liqueur – Grand Marnier or Poire William – to taste to the basic crème anglaise.

This is the basis used for the raspberry soufflé on page 166. Use frozen raspberries for the purée. They're moister and cheaper than fresh raspberries.
Blackberries can be substituted for the raspberries. They need less water – 25 ml (1 fl oz) instead of 100 ml (3½ fl oz) – and you should use Crème de Cassis instead of the Framboise.

RASPBERRY REDUCTION

MAKES ABOUT 400 ML (14 FL OZ)

*500 ml (17 fl oz) raspberry purée, sieved
15 g (½ oz) cornflour
25 ml (1 fl oz) Framboise (raspberry eau de vie)
100 g (4 oz) caster sugar   100 ml (3½ fl oz) water*

1. Put the raspberry purée in a pan and simmer very gently to reduce it by half.
2. Dissolve the cornflour in the Framboise, and add this to the reduced purée. Stir and cook until thickened, then remove from the heat.

3. Mix the sugar and water together in a separate pan and boil up to 121°C/250°F. Add to the raspberry mixture and mix in well. Leave to cool, then use as the base for the soufflé on page 166.

RASPBERRY COULIS

This simple but delicious sauce can be made a day or so in advance. It can also be frozen. Make a blackberry coulis in exactly the same way.

4 PORTIONS

300 g (11 oz) fresh raspberries
100 g (4 oz) caster sugar

1. Place the raspberries in a bowl and cover with the sugar. Leave them macerating for a while so that the sugar can begin pulling out the fruit juices.

2. Place the raspberries and sugar in a mixer or blender, and blend to a purée.
3. Pass through a fine sieve to catch all the seeds, and the coulis is ready. Chill before use.

PASSIONFRUIT SAUCE

An aromatic sauce for the Champagne Jelly on page 150. It's good with a few other desserts as well.

4-6 PORTIONS

250 g (9 oz) passionfruit pulp (about 12 fruit)
30 g (1¼ oz) caster sugar   1 tablespoon water
3 tablespoons fresh orange juice
85 ml (3 fl oz) Stock Syrup (SEE BELOW)

1. Put the passionfruit pulp and seeds in a saucepan with the caster sugar and water. Bring the mixture to the boil and simmer for 2-3 minutes.

2. Liquidise the mixture briefly then pass it through a fine sieve, leaving the seeds behind.
3. Add the juice and syrup to the sieved pulp, and bring to the boil. Skim, sieve and cool.

STOCK SYRUP

Useful in a number of ways - in sauces, for fruit, and as a constituent of a sorbet mix.

MAKES ABOUT 900 ML (1½ PINTS)

450 g (1 lb) caster sugar
600 ml (1 pint) water

1. Dissolve the sugar in the water by bringing to the boil slowly, stirring to ensure all the sugar dissolves.

2. Continue to boil the syrup for 1 minute.
3. Sieve, cool and store in a screw-top jar in a cool place.

Use this delicious mincemeat in all the traditional Christmas ways, but it's particularly good as the stuffing for a baked apple (see page 174).

MINCEMEAT

MAKES A GOOD 1.5-1.75 KG (2½-3 LB)

200 g (7 oz) beef suet
200 g (7 oz) raisins   200 g (7 oz) currants
200 g (7 oz) grated apple   100 g (4 oz) sultanas
80 g (3¼ oz) soft brown sugar
60 g (2¼ oz) mixed peel
4 pinches each of ground cinnamon and grated nutmeg
4 cloves
finely grated zest of 4 lemons
200 ml (7 fl oz) dark rum
200 ml (7 fl oz) brandy

1. Combine all the dry ingredients in a large bowl, mixing well to distribute the spices.
2. Add the rum and brandy and mix well again.

3. Pot in clean dry jars, cover with wax circles and a top, and leave for at least a few days (and up to a couple of months) to mature.

A useful garnish for desserts — and an occasional meat dish. Prepare at least the day before.

CONFIT OF CITRUS ZEST

zest of 1 orange, 2 limes or 2 lemons (or a mixture)
Stock Syrup to cover (SEE OPPOSITE)

1. Cut the citrus zest into very thin julienne strips and blanch briefly in boiling water. Refresh in cold water.
2. Repeat this blanching and refreshing twice more, to get rid of any bitterness. Drain very thoroughly.

3. Place the zest julienne in a small pan with just enough stock syrup to cover. Bring to the boil, then cook gently until the zest is tender, about 20 minutes.
4. Leave to cool in the syrup. When required, drain off the surplus syrup.

This is used as a specific garnish for the White Chocolate Mousse on page 159, but it could happily accompany many other dishes. It keeps well.

ORANGE CONFIT

2 oranges, washed and thinly sliced
400 g (14 oz) caster sugar   200 ml (7 fl oz) water

1. Preheat the oven to 100°C/212°F/the very lowest gas.
2. Bring the sugar and water to the boil together in a saucepan to melt the sugar, then take off the heat and leave for a few minutes to cool marginally.

3. Place the orange slices in an ovenproof tray, and pour the syrup over just to cover. Put into the preheated oven for about 1½ hours.
4. Remove from the oven and leave the orange slices to cool in the liquor. Store in the syrup, but drain the slices to serve.

INDEX

garlic: confit of garlic, 207
gazpacho of crab, 22
goat's cheese, ravioli of, 28
grapefruit: gratin d'Agrumes, 170
gratin d'Agrumes, 170
gratinée of salt cod, 81
grouse, roast, 118-19

haddock *see* smoked haddock
ham: grilled salmon, 89
    roast ham with a bittersweet port
      wine sauce, 128
    terrine d'hiver, 49-51
haricot beans: cassoulette of monk-
    fish, 67
hazelnuts: nougat glacé, 154
herbs: fromage blanc with, 214
    soft herb crust, 214
Hollandaise sauce, 202

ice cream: nougat glacé, 154
    vanilla, 181

jellies: champagne, 150
    Madeira, 194
    red wine, 148
John Dory with endive, 76
juniper berries: juniper berry butter
    sauce, 201
    juniper jus, 196
jus of thyme, 197-8
jus rôti, 195

lamb: best end of lamb, 129
    lamb stock sauce, 191
    roast rump of lamb, 132
    roast saddle of lamb, 130
    roast saddle of lamb forestière,
      134-5
langoustines, ravioli of, 29
lasagne of cod, 80
leeks: vichyssoise, 21
lentilles du pays, 212
lettuce, braised, 210
lime jus, 198
liqueur crème Anglaise, 219
liver: chicken liver and foie gras
    parfait, 57-8
    escalope of calf's liver, 143-4

Madeira jelly, 194
Madeira sauce, 194-5
magret of duck, 111
marquise de chocolat, 183-4
Mascarpone: iced tiramisu parfait,
    155
    tiramisu, 156
mayonnaise, 204
meat, 103
    see also individual types of meat
meringue: oeufs à la neige, 188

vacherin of red fruits, 151
mincemeat, 221
    baked apple, 174
mint: sauce paloise, 202
monkfish: cassoulette of, 67
    roast monkfish with braised
      squid, 68
mousses: champagne, 160-2
    chicken, 214
    white chocolate, 159
mushrooms: cappuccino of, 17
    fillet of beef forestière, 137
    mushroom duxelles, 215
    roast saddle of lamb forestière,
      134-5
    terrine d'hiver, 49-51
mussel soup, 18
mustard: mustard beurre blanc,
    203
    sabayon of grain mustard, 199

nougat glacé, 154

oeufs à la neige, 188
oeufs meurette, 30
olives: magret of duck, 111
    tapenade, 206
onions, roast, 207
opéra, 186-7
orange: gratin d'Agrumes, 170
    orange confit, 221
oxtail, braised, in crépinette, 140-1
oysters: marinated salmon with
    deep-fried oysters, 39
    with champagne sabayon, 35

parfait, iced tiramisu, 155
partridge, choucroûte of, 116-17
passionfruit: sauce, 220
    sorbet, 170
pasta: fresh pasta, 215
    lasagne of cod, 80
    ravioli of goat's cheese, 28
    ravioli of langoustine, 29
pastry: puff, 215-16
    sweet, 216
pâtés: chicken liver and foie gras
    parfait, 57-8
pears: tarte Bourdaloue, 177
peppercorns: skate au poivre, 71
peppers: gazpacho of crab, 22
    ratatouille, 212-13
pigeon, roast wood, 121-4
pineapple cream, sweet and sour,
    201
pomme Anna, 208
pomme fondant, 208
pomme rösti, 209
pomme sablé, 207
pomme sauté, 209
pork: cabbage à l'Ancienne, 54

roast suckling pig, 127
port: bittersweet port wine sauce,
    197
    sauce aigre-doux, 197
potatoes: pomme Anna, 208
    pomme fondant, 208
    pomme rösti, 209
    pomme sablé, 207
    pomme sauté, 209
    vichyssoise, 21
poultry, 103
puddings, 145-88
puff pastry, 215-16

quail, roast, 107-8

rabbit, roast ballotine of, 125
raspberries: raspberry coulis, 220
    raspberry reduction, 219-20
    raspberry sorbet, 151
    raspberry soufflé, 166
ratatouille, 212-13
ravioli: goat's cheese, 28
    langoustine, 29
red mullet: with couscous, coulis of
    red pepper, 94
    with beignets of sage, sauce
      vièrge, 93
rhubarb tart, 181
rice *see* risotto
risotto: of ink, 24
    of sea scallops, 27
rösti, 209

sabayon: of grain mustard, 199
    sweet sabayon, 218
sage, beignets of, 213
salads: tuna Niçoise, 45
salmon: ballotine of salmon, 40
    compote of salmon, 42
    fresh salmon, pomme sauté, 86
    grilled darne of salmon, 90
    grilled salmon, 89
    marinated salmon with deep-fried
      oysters, 39
    salmon confit, 88
salt cod: gratinée of salt cod, 81
    soup of brandade, 19
sauces: aigre-doux, 197
    Béarnaise, 202
    beurre blanc, 203
    bittersweet port wine, 197
    caramel, 218
    citrus butter, 201-2
    crème Anglaise, 219
    diable, 196
    double chicken butter, 203
    gazpacho, 205
    gribiche, 205
    Hollandaise, 202
    juniper berry butter, 201